CALLING FROM KASHGAR

For Alice and Ruth

CALLLING FROM KASHGAR

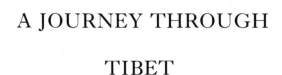

A JOURNEY THROUGH

TIBET

Rod Richard

First Published 1990
Frontier Publishing.
Windetts. Kirstead. Norfolk.
NR15 1BR

British Library C I P data
Richard, Rod 1950-
    Calling from Kashgar : a journey through Tibet.
    1. Tibet : Visitors' guides
    I. Title
    915.105459

ISBN 0-9508701-7-X

PRINTED IN GREAT BRITAIN
by F. Crowe & Sons, Norwich.

CONTENTS

INTRODUCTION

Travel in China has long held a fascination for many from the very different culture of Western Europe dating back to the remarkable travels of Marco Polo in the 13th century.

After this brief flurry of contact, however, China again retired behind its bamboo curtain for several centuries.

The rise of European trade and naval power altered this first with the Portuguese at Macao in the 16th century. By 1840 the Opium War between Britain and China had destroyed China's attempts to keep her borders inviolate and opened the way for a series of unequal treaties which the Europeans, and later the Americans and Japanese, exploited to China's disadvantage.

This exploitation was not simply in terms of trade, but also in exposing a largely unwilling population to competing missionary influences. That is not to suggest that much of the missionary work was not of a high standard and bought many tangible benefits to the people, including Western medicine, hygiene and moves against widespread corruption.

Many of the written accounts of China in the 19th and 20th centuries come from these missionary sources, and not a few of them undertook remarkable journeys and penetrated to remote and inaccessible parts of the Empire. It provided for them a *raison d'être* for their travels which is now rarely the case, so other less readily defined justifications have to be sought – if indeed justification for travel is necessary at all.

China travel has also traditionally been hampered by governments in disarray, competing factions of warlords, disputes over regional autonomy, religious or ethnic minorities, and political dogmas. With the 1911 Revolution the Chinese Empire fell apart and was to remain in turmoil until the Communist victory of 1949. Since then periods of consolidation have been set back by a series of mass movements, which have spread confusion and disruption in their wake. The Cultural Revolution of 1966–76 saw this process reach its apogee in what is now largely accepted by Chinese and others alike to have been an unprecedented national disaster from which it will take decades for the self inflicted wounds and the shattered economy to recover.

China has, however, a great cultural heritage. Its natural resources are impressive, though these are constantly under pressure from its vast and growing population. The many positive achievements of the Communist Revolution also cannot be dismissed lightly. With the reopening of relations with the West after the period of introspection that followed 1949, China has become a fascinating melting pot of ideas old and new where the pace of change is ever accelerating.

One facet of this has been easier access for foreigners, a developing tourist industry and a lessening of official paranoia about external influences. It has also been seen as a very good way of obtaining foreign exchange recognised in the issue of Foreign Exchange Certificates (FEC) in 1979. It was from this year that first a trickle, but before long a flood of foreigners started to visit, reaching even some of the remoter areas that had been entirely cut off from scrutiny for three decades.

Initially only a very limited number of major cities and tourist attractions were open to foreign travellers, and Aliens Travel Permits were required for all but these open areas. Rapidly this changed and by 1986 travel permits had generally become redundant. China is a very large country and there are still areas that remain closed. These may be for military/security reasons as on the frontier with Vietnam, or for nuclear installations in the Lop Nor Basin. They may also be because of internal disorder, for instance, some Muslim areas in Xinjiang or Minority groups in South-West China.

China is understandably a little reticent about its Minorities' policies after serious cultural and religious repression. This is particularly true of Tibet and was one of the major reasons for wanting to keep foreigners out, and so the world largely in a state of ignorance as to the true state of affairs. Some of the first visitors to Lhasa in 1979 appear to have been chosen because of the sympathetic picture they would paint in thanks for being allowed the privilege of a visit.

Unfortunately for the Chinese authorities this new openness has not all been entirely to their liking, with the

Tibetans tasting at last a little more freedom and demanding very much more. This contributed to riots in Lhasa in 1987 with a resulting clamp down. Perhaps Paul Theroux's most telling comment on his travels from 'Riding the Iron Rooster', is, 'in order to understand the Chinese you have to visit Tibet' – a sad reflection, though, on China's uneasy relationship with her neighbour, in particular since 1959. The history of relations between China and Tibet is a complex one. China claims sovereignty. Tibet has at worst conceded Chinese suzerainty. In the short term this may simply be academic as the one point on which the Chinese are quite clear, is that sovereignty is now non-negotiable and they hold all the cards. In the long term Tibetan nationalistic aspirations cannot be ignored, but it may well be that the joint effects of colonisation and tourism may undermine Tibetan culture in a fashion that straightforward military invasion, domination and suppression could never do. China now reluctantly refers to 'errors' and 'excesses' in the handling of the Tibetan question, as if, by so doing they have gone far enough to atone for the attempted cultural and national genocide of a claimed part of their own empire. Tiananmen Square may have caused some to pause and consider when they do unto their own that which they have done unto others. However, we should not condemn a nation, or specifically a race within that nation, albeit that they constitute 90% of the whole, for atrocities carried out. Do we really get the government we deserve? Have the Han Chinese deserved theirs? Sadly one cannot escape from greater Han chauvinism, their tendency to treat others as less than full citizens, and therefore somehow deserving of harsh treatment.

I came to Tibet largely by accident having travelled through China and acquired, I thought, some understanding of their language and culture. I had found much I had enjoyed and admired. I had made some friends. I had been greatly entertained, amused and mentally stimulated.

Tibet forced me to reconsider, both in philosophical and political terms, where I stood. It became apparent to me I could not sit endlessly on the fence. For the Chinese to mend their fences in Tibet requires more than a few half-hearted apologies followed by the reimposition of martial law.

The journey I undertook through West Tibet, which at no time in history has been officially open to foreign travel, is again not likely to be achieved easily over the next few years.

My travels in eastern China in retrospect were excellent training for Tibet, and having found that Lhasa was now firmly on the tour group map I was encouraged to push out west precisely because it offered uncertainty and challenges other than a degree of patience in the face of bureaucratic intransigence. Much of China travel is slow uncomfortable and frustrating. As Alexandra David-Neal recalls, 'a full account of the days spent in argument would sound like an epic poem of olden days, half comic, half sad.' Travel through West Tibet to Kashgar epitomised this, and also carried with it the extra edge of the illicit, the danger of arrest and ignominioius deportation.

Before setting out for China I had had no idea of visiting Tibet. Although it held a mystical fascination since childhood, a land different from all others, it had not occured to me that it might be visited with comparitive ease. I was but barely aware of the history of exploration. I had heard of Sven Hedin, Heinrich Harrer and Younghusband. I knew ' nothing of Manning, Bouvalot, Prince Henri d'Orleans, Dutreuil de Rhins, Annie Taylor, Mrs Littledale, Susie Rijnhart, to name but a few.

On my return home I have discovered a whole new world of armchair travelling, but most of all I find myself changed not only by the experience of travel, but quite specifically but inexplicably by Mt Kailas, the remote Holy Buddhist mountain in West Tibet, which has since held a vivid place in both my dreams and waking hours, that forces me into constant reassessment of its significance. This was not so apparent at the time, but I know that this is not simply a romanticisation after the event, a self-fulfilling prophecy, although my journey there was by accident rather than design.

Rod Richard. Nairn, February 1990.

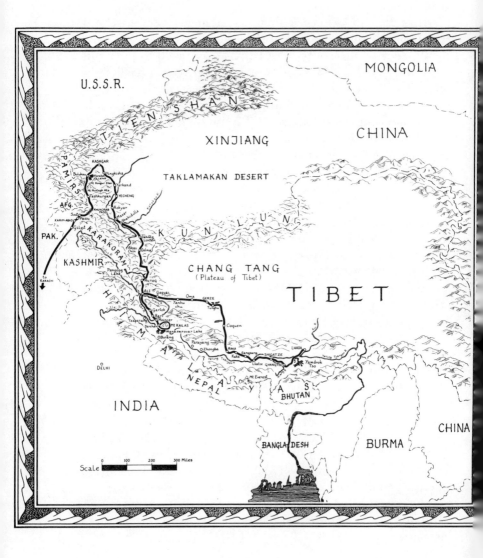

1

CITY OF ETERNAL
SPRING

September 21st 1986 – Kings Cross Station – these days
more like an airport with its coloured plastics and high-tech
information systems. No longer has it quite the sense of great
departures, gateway to the north, wreathed in clouds of
steam. It felt more like yet another entrepot for processing
packaged humanity. I joined a ticket office queue. We
moved forward. "A second class single nightrider to
Edinburgh, please." "That's £17.50 – leaves 2200 –
platform 10." "Thanks."

Dazed, mouth agape, I hesitated, shouldered my rucksack
and turned away in confusion. Was this a dream? Could it
really be so simple? No argument, no haggling over price,
availability, my status – practically no waiting.

Call this a queue. Seven months earlier on March 5th 1986
I flew from Gatwick to Hong Kong, a moment I had been
waiting for for years. Although I had last been in Hong
Kong in 1972 I had never given up the hope in the
intervening years that I might someday return and realise
my ambition of seeing something of the Chinese mainland.
In 1972 this was simply not possible. The Cultural
Revolution was at its height. Practically no foreigners
entered the country and a British regular army officer
studying Chinese at University, as I was at the time, was
hardly likely to have been one of the chosen few. I had to
content myself with gazing out over the border from Crest
Hill observation post several hundred feet above the railway
crossing at Lo Hu. This was an odd vantage point from
which to view another country. With the aid of telescopes,
binoculars and donkey's ears the whole experience was
peculiarly voyeuristic. At the time the border was very
active, but this did not affect my static week at Crest Hill. I

was never quite clear what we were supposed to do if a few million of the People's Liberation Army swarmed across the border. Fight to the last man presumably, but at least we had a telephone on which to cry "help". From what I have seen subsequently this would not have been a happy time to have made China's acquaintance.

A couple of days in Hong Kong and I had adjusted to the first culture shock and prepared for the great leap forward into China. I arrived at Guangzhou (Canton) at 7 a.m. off the night ferry, quickly cleared Chinese customs, changed some money and marched out through the main doorway into the Chinese morning. From what I'd made of the map, left seemed like the right direction, so I set off up the street feeling very unreal. I think this is partly because of having no idea what to expect. Arrival in Guangzhou in retrospect is so like so much of China. It is neither a magical old China of coolie hats, pigtails, junks and carved wooden houses, nor is it all smart modern concrete, machinery and fashion. It is, of course, a mix of all these elements. One of the things that struck me most forcefully was that the picture I had held of a uniform society, if ever wholly true, was now rapidly disappearing. On my first day in the People's Republic my former illusions were shattered. I think many Europeans of my generation, veering to the left, had looked at Russian communism and been easily convinced that in that direction salvation did not lie. Meanwhile the pure agrarian revolution in China could be held up as an ideal. Since at the time remarkably little was known about China and practically no one was able to visit, this vision could be fairly safely maintained.

These thoughts, however, had to be put to one side for the time being as I reached a major junction and made my first attempt to converse in Chinese. I had studied Chinese for two years at Cambridge from 1971 to 1973, but had no opportunity in the intervening years to use what little I had mastered at that time. I had consequently started again from scratch a couple of months before departing for China. I was constantly astonished by how selective my memory was. Even in lesson two of the new text book I had acquired I was confronted with a character I was convinced I had never seen

12

before. At other times I found I recognised something quite obscure, maybe from a classical text I had ploughed my way through. Reassuringly my opening gambit half worked and I managed to board a bus in the right direction, encouragement to persevere.

The most major shock to the system is Chinese noise, incessant, at first overpowering, and I wondered how people could live with it without going rapidly insane. In time I too came to live with it.

My original plan had been to travel directly north to Kaifeng in Henan Province to visit my cousin Liz McLeod who had since September been teaching English at Henan University, but the lure of South-West China was too great and I resolved to make a south-western circuit first. Consequently I took all the essential goods I had been instructed to bring out from England, like marmite, shampoo and running socks, and had these neatly packed into a little wooden box and posted off.

This visit to the post office was another exciting linguistic challenge and I discovered how much easier it is to retain language when it has been used for a real purpose. In Western universities you only ever see Chinese characters when you open a book, or occasionally outside the Chinese take-away. In China you are assailed by characters on all sides. Once learned every street sign is a confirmation everytime you step outside, an invitation to investigation and learning. You begin to live characters, maybe to sleep and dream them too. Even some forms of runninghand, the equivalent of handwriting rather than block printing, become recognisable. This began to afford me the greatest pleasure. The sight of all these characters made me reassess the importance of written language as a medium and the feel it gives to a country. This was to strike me very forcibly later moving through Tibet, Pakistan and Turkey. Turkey in particular surprised me because I had expected an Arabic script. The sight of street signs, advertising, etc., in Roman script made the country seem very much more western than eastern. This visual effect is quite separate from the actual sounds represented by the various different written forms.

From Guangzhou I travelled again by boat up the Pearl

13

River to Wuzhou. It carried about eight hundred passengers on the three decks, on each deck two levels of bunks. These were in fact just continuous sleeping platforms down both sides with wooden slats between – sufficient to lie down, but little more. It has rather unfairly been described as concentration camp accommodation. I, in fact, found this a most leisurely way to travel, though no doubt it would become unbearably hot later in the year. All the foreigners, about twenty-five, had been place in one line in what appeared to be prime position; topdeck, top row, port side, at the bow furthest from the dubious toilets. This struck me as an inspired piece of administration, as most of these tickets had been bought in ones and two over the previous couple of days.

At this early stage in China travel there was definitely safety in numbers. Adjusting to being stared at constantly is something no one finds entirely easy. Here we were in sufficient strength to stare back, and with the open plan arrangements mutual observation helped the hours pass by. One of the factors of this mode of travel is that you meet new people with whom there is an openness, maybe initially desperation, that you would never experience in such brief encounters in your own country. You may therefore only travel with someone for a few hours, but the meeting will have left a lasting impression.

These large numbers, packed on board like sardines, reminded me of the disaster on a ferry in northern China. A fight broke out, and with natural overwhelming curiosity everyone rushed over to watch. The boat then capsized and a hundred and forty drowned. The man held responsible for starting the fight survived, but was later shot. I had thought at the time that the story was somewhat improbable, but having now witnessed crowd behaviour and shipboard life it no longer seemed surprising.

From Wuzhou the bus to Yangshuo took eight hours, for the most part winding slowly through hilly countryside sparsely covered in pines, with rice paddies levelled out on terraces on every possible piece of low lying ground.

Yangshuo is about two hours bus ride from Guilin which has now become a major tourist centre. Prices have risen accordingly and I had been warned it suffered from all the worst excesses of the attempt to attract and cater for the tour group market. In contrast Yangshuo is a delightful small town with a busy market, which despite the bustle of life has a sleepy atmosphere to it in rhythm with the slowly flowing water of the Li River. Already in March it was hot, humid and generally hazy. Everyday this tranquil atmosphere is disrupted, however, by the arrival of the tour group boats from Guilin. About half an hour before they arrive the waterfront is filled with hastily occupied stalls solely to cater for this trade. The tourists have just long enough to purchase their souvenirs before boarding a fleet of minibuses that roar out of town with horns blaring. Five minutes later the chickens have stopped squawking, the dust has settled, the stall holders have melted away, and life returns to normal.

One of the most attractive features of Yangshuo from the traveller's point of view was that bicycles for hire were cheap and readily available. In so many places the lack of transport, or the prohibitive cost of minibuses, usually reserved exclusively for big hotel tour groups, meant that it was difficult to venture very far from city centres. Fortunately the authorities by 1986 seemed to be getting slightly less paranoid about foreigners careering around the rice paddies and so I was able to ride out to Moon Hill, stopping en route to admire a fisherman operating precariously from a floating log. About him shimmered the reflections of bizarre limestone pillars rising vertically out of the paddie fields. I had always believed that Chinese landscape painting was largely a projection of the imagination. The actuality around Yangshuo belies this theory.

From Yangshuo a bus took me to Guilin and a chance walk-on flight to Kunming. So far I realised the accommodation nightmare had been only preliminary skirmishing. At the Kunming Hotel I was to meet the full force of counter clerk intransigence. It's a mystery why they always go through with this nuisance factor. It makes no difference to the staff what price of accommodation you take. There are no financial incentives. They have no vested interest in the profitability of the hotel. It all smacks of petty bureaucrats exercising their limited power to the maximum for lack of any other opportunities in otherwise rigidly controlled lives. All this can rapidly lead to an increase in blood pressure as can frequently be witnessed at booking counters throughout the land. Patience I have been told is a virtue, but sadly not one of my strong points. For the preservation of sanity I was having to acquire some very quickly. In time I came quite to enjoy these little cameos, endlessly repeated arrival performances. Unrolling your sleeping bag in the foyer can work wonders.

Kunming, the capital of Yunnan Province, with a population of three million, sits at the head of the Dian Lake, 6,000 feet above sea level. Although its 'Spring City' adage tends to be overstated (it actually snowed in February) the climate is very agreeable. Visible from the city centre are the Western Hills and a ring of mountains to the north. Nothing spectacular, but with the Dian Lake to the south it has variety and a natural beauty. Yunnan has more minority groups than any other province and these help to lend a colourful atmosphere to Kunming that tempers the conformist austerity of the Han Chinese.

There is a fair concentration of medium to heavy industry. Students of English, invariably reared for some reason on Dickens, always ask about London fog. Although I remember this vaguely as a child, no English city can now compete with Chinese ones for belching clouds of smoke. Although by no means the worst, Kunming is no exception, with the result that black dust is all pervasive and the avid joggers in the European community, whom I was shortly to meet, complained that they could only safely run very early in the morning in order to avoid silicosis. China T.V. recently serialised 'Hard Times' and 'Our Mutual Friend' which Chinese students found compulsive viewing. I think they found it easy to identify with the foggy atmosphere, street life and a strong puritanical morality pitched against the evils of corruption. Later exposed to this bizarre spectacle, I found British actors in top hats dubbed into Chinese a little hard to take seriously, even when I could follow the story line.

Unlike many other cities Kunming has not gone very far along the road of modernisation. Despite an incredible amount of building activity, large sections of the old city, with overhanging eaves, intricate carved doors and windows with peeling red and green paint still remain. The bustling markets recently re-established give the feel more of the old China than of the present day.

Bicycles are the prime mode of transport. Buses are incredibly cheap, about 1p for most city rides, but you usually have to fight your way on board and the bus then has to fight its way down the street through a sea of bicycles floating back and forth. With a bicycle you have independence. Most Chinese cyclists progress at a stately pace. Foreigners inclined to force the pace or out joy riding in the countryside are regarded as a menace. There is maybe something in this in that the mechanics are seldom up to standard and brake failures are common. The first action in buying a new bike, I was advised, is to take it to the bicycle repair man to have all the nuts and bolts tightened. When I became the proud owner of a 'Spring Flower' bike I duly followed this wise counsel. Accidents are common. The accidents themselves are seldom serious, but the crowd-pulling abuse that follows can develop into quite vicious fights, always a popular spectacle.

Before leaving for China I spent a month in London gaining a preparatory TEFL certificate. I had no clear idea of finding employment on this trip, just felt it might open up new avenues. I had no intention of commiting myself to a couple of years in some grim industrial northern city. At this stage I was happy to investigate, to put out tentative feelers. My enquiries lead to a surprise visit from Jeremy *(Zhao Zhenming)*, the Yunnan University waiban or liaison officer. Half an hour later I had been signed up for three months as a replacement Foreign Expert to teach English to the Attached Middle School *(YunDa Fushu Waiyu Xuexiao)*. This school was made up of the best middle school students from the whole province. Having their own foreign teacher was an

17

exceptional investment for 15 to 17 year olds, and an awesome responsibility for my first ever teaching post.

I soon came to understand how my predecessor had come to leave in total exasperation. Immediate employment meant ten days of bureaucratic delays, while my passport was lodged with Public Security. This meant I could not leave Kunming to visit Dali or Xishuangbanna as many of my fellow travellers had done. I was suffering from a slight identity crisis. I had just been getting into my stride as a traveller and here I was stopped dead in my tracks. However this seemed like an opportunity not to be missed. I could find out whether or not I liked teaching and I would have a chance to see a side of life that is largely a closed book when you are travelling.

In the intervening week I kept myself well entertained with the sights of Kunming and the immediate surrounding area. Vodka, the aptly transliterated *edeke*, being basically colourless, odourless and tasteless is probably the safest spirit to abuse in China besides being one of the cheapest. When not recovering from such excesses I rose early. This is usually not too difficult as Chinese life bursts into noisy action at 6am. In the central square large crowds, mainly made up of the elderly, gather for Tai Ch'i. On some mornings a couple of athletic girls performed Wu Shu sword drills. Another group of elderly waved red hankerchiefs to slow motion shuffling, peculiarly reminiscent of Morris dancing.

Part of the Tai Ch'i was a deep breathing exercise for the abdomen. The spectacle of two *waiguoren*, of which I was one, joining in, considerably enlivened the proceedings to the extent that I feared a few ancients might get terminally carried away. This was a very warm and accepting sharing of simple humanity.

I started teaching before either a visa had been issued or accommodation arranged. I was not in fact to receive a temporary residence permit until May, sometime after my original visa had expired. Two days after I started Jeremy turned up to give me the limousine treatment to transport my luggage, one rucksack, up to the university accommodation.

Having one's own flat is an almost unheard of luxury in China. I occupied the space usually allocated to a whole extended family, about which I often felt rather guilty, but at the same time relieved. Privacy is an alien concept to the Chinese. I have always been a fairly gregarious person, but found in China that I positively welcomed a fair measure of my own company.

My flat had a small concrete kitchen with fridge, a bedroom, sitting room, a balcony at either end and a shower and lavatory ingeniously designed so that you could only sit on it with the door open and your feet sticking out into the sitting room. This suggested the plumbing facilities had been planned with foreign teachers in mind, but no practical experience of the device's modus operandi. In the kitchen there was a fiendish heating and cooking stove that ran on cylindrical shaped coal blocks with holes bored through them. It made Rayburn management seem like simplicity itself. Once alight they operate quite satisfactorily, but lighting them was never successfully mastered by any of the foreign teachers. We frequently had to enlist each other's aid in transferring burning coals from one stove to another which required some deft tongs work. They also helped contribute to the already dust laden atmosphere in turning all surfaces black. After a while I acquired a *dianlu* a small electric ring, which made me less dependent on the stove, but forced more often into cold showers.

The other block where some of the teaching staff were billetted had been surrounded by a wall with a gate and gate house. Gatekeeper is one of the jobs fundamental to Chinese society. Many gateways, seemingly of little importance, provide employment, a *raison d'être* for countless throughout the land. It is, of course, also a very effective way of policing the community. In this sense the gatekeeper holds considerable power. Little happens that is not observed and reported on. As part of a new building project this wall was demolished. The gate, however, remained standing and for a couple of days afterwards the gatekeeper rose religiously at six to open the gate and ceremoniously closed it again at 11.30 p.m. His actions were not so much a matter of old habits die hard as the fact that no new regulations had been issued. He could not be criticised for carrying out the existing ones.

This mentality was by no means confined to the gate-keeping classes. On one occasion I covered for the MA English course. According to Kim, their Canadian teacher, his class divided into three groups. One was a small group of hardline Maoists. Although temporarily eclipsed, they held rigid views which not so long previously had been very much in vogue. They mistrusted the new more open China. For them interpretation of Western literature was difficult for the basic premise was that it was all decadent and ideo-logically unsound. It was also difficult to reconcile being a Maoist and a student, as Mao had condemned all intellectuals as 'the stinking ninth' category, placed in the same company as spies, traitors and capitalist roaders.

The middle ground was held by the majority. They were stimulated by the rapidly changing scene, but at the same time fundamentally cautious. Any opinions expressed were carefully hedged, and usually capped with a safe party line. The third group could not wait to exploit all the new opportunities. They despised the austerity of the past. They were young, this was their world. They intended to enjoy it to the full.

I read the first pieces completed during a free composition hour. One girl's submission was particularly revealing. Although she did not identify herself, the piece was obviously autobiographical. She had been at the weekend to visit an old schoolfriend who by local standards had recently amassed a small fortune as a successful entrepreneur.

"I said to him," she wrote, "are you not worried about what will happen if the policy changes?"

He replied, "I know that tall trees catch the wind, but I don't think it's wrong to make money by my own hard work. I can't do otherwise."

In other words, whatever shall be shall be. The wind may change but he firmly belonged to the school of 'live now, maybe pay later'.

She concluded with a rather pompous line, "but as us intellectuals know, these kind of people often exploit their own children to get rich and take them away from schooling." Throughout, however, her admiration for the man was patently obvious. She belonged to the middle ground, but at heart aspired to the racy world of money and the rewards that this can now bring. There is a very definite age divide. The vast majority of intellectuals over the age of thirty had been so scarred by the Cultural Revolution that they were pathologically incapable of expressing their own opinion. This assumption that there must be a correct line made seminar teaching very difficult. Students were simply not geared to carrying out their own work, they wanted to be told the official line. One of Kim's greatest complaints was that a very great deal of any submitted written work was plagiarised, usually lifted, whole paragraphs, if not pages at a time. A tedious business having to go through all this pointing out the page references.

Fortunately my students, 15 to 17 year olds, still had the fresh inquisitiveness of youth. For them the Cultural Revolution was not part of their own life experience. They witnessed its lasting effects on their parents generation, but like the post-war children in Europe it was no longer the dominant factor. Theirs was a new age, for China a new dawning. They were among the privileged few, the vanguard, the Young Pioneers, who fully expected to inherit the earth. My task therefore promised to be very much less frustrating.

In retrospect after the destruction of so much hope in Tiananmen Square on June 4th 1989, I wonder how many of these students still hold the same optimism about the future.

2

OUT OF TOWN

During my three and a half months in Kunming I had the good fortune to make trips out to Xishuangbanna and Dali, as well as a two day solo bike ride round the Dian Lake, memorable for immediately getting lost and as a result enjoying some unexpected village life.

In April the foreign community were invited by the Yunnan Foreign Affairs Bureau *(waiban)* to go on a trip to Xishuangbanna, an autonomous district at the very southern end of the country, bordering with Laos and Burma. In recent years the autonomous regions and districts have begun to enjoy a little more freedom with the return of some religious toleration and the development of a freer market economy. In reality though, control is firmly maintained by the Han Chinese, and any minority leaders are for the most part puppets or mere figureheads. Thus although the government have made much of a more open minority's policy, it remains to be seen whether actions will match the rhetoric. In the present climate of reasserted central control this seems highly unlikely.

Jinghong the capital on the Mekong *(Langcan)* river is also the old capital of the Dai minority. They number about 850,000 and are spread out through Laos, Thailand, Burma and China. In language, culture and race they are more akin to the Thais and Vietnamese than the Chinese, the people, it is alleged, having been driven south in the 13th century by the Mongol invasion. The society is strongly Buddhist, maintaining a distinctive character of its own. This is partly because of its inaccessability. The main road in from Simao was only constructed in the '60's.

Xishuangbanna is sub-tropical. The houses are built on stilts with pigs rooting about underneath. Palms and banana trees grow in the compounds. The bright colours of the native dress are set against a mass of bougainvillia blossom. There is a sense of leisure and tranquility that is not so evident in the hustle and bustle of Kunming city life.

The flight from Kunming to Simao took an hour and a half in a forty seat Russian Antonov. Below scudded bright green rice paddies terraced up the valley sides to be outlined sharply against the burnt brown scrubby hills. Altogether this is a very confused and jumbled up landscape, in which several different Minority groups live pretty much cut off from the outside world. Because of the very poor communications the Chinese government have experienced difficulty in exercising effective control over these areas. Only since 1985 have you no longer needed a hard-to-obtain travel permit to Xishuangbanna, and although not strictly enforced this is usually interpreted as being for JingHong only. Until they began to realise its tourist potential, the Han could see no reason why anyone would want to visit what they clearly regarded as a backward Minority area.

From Simao it is a six hour minibus ride winding at alarming speed along narrow roads with dense jungle vegetation closing in on both sides, at times forming a gloomy, lightless tunnel. Consequently for much of the journey the view is distinctly limited. Because Kunming sits at 6,000 feet, its climate belies its southern position. Dropping down into Xishuangbanna the feel is quite different – hot, humid, exotic smells, exotic plants, exotic people. At the end of the drive you finally emerge from the hills to look down on the Mekong river, muddy and swift flowing. It is not so much impressive in itself but for all its associations with the Vietnam war. Laos is just down river and Vietnam only a country away.

The object of the visit was to witness the Water Splashing Festival *(Po shui jie)* which takes place at the Dai new year, around the middle of April. This year it was the start of the year 1348, the Dai choosing to follow their own history rather than a chronology based on a man from another time and place. Many of us would have preferred to make our own arrangements rather than travelling in a large shepherded tour group, but transport was at a premium, particularly for

23

the festival and as a result this was the most difficult time of year to get there. I would have very much liked to have got out of JingHong down river on the Mekong to Gan Lan Ban, but it immediately became obvious that the waiban accompanying us had strict instructions not to let us do anything of the sort. This was a very good object lesson in the fact that when travelling as an individual in China, all sorts of things are possible, as long as you have endless patience and a will to succeed. Once you hand over responsibility for your movements and accommodation to any form of group organiser you either have to accept sheep status or serious attacks of apoplexy.

The *Po shui jie* was a day of magnificent pageantry. Everyone was in town for the dragon boat races. For the girls in particular this is the day to be seen, parading with parasols in all their finery, the Dai in bright saris and bodices, and a host of little known minority groups each in their own distinctive dress. The most outstanding of these were four sisters identically dressed in black with tall white hats and the minimum of ornamentation, the effect quite stunning, and they knew it. In much of Han China the feel is of a near sexless society. Maybe times have simply been too hard for there to be much energy to spare for romance, but here it is fundamental to the Dai way of life. It is not just the girls. The male dragon boat crews exuded an almost macho like self-confidence.

From a large stand on top of the river bank over a hundred yards down to the water was a mass of seething humanity; food stalls, medical posts, elephants foot drum dancers, rocketeers, dragon boat crews and a liberal supply of photographers carrying equipment equivalent to several years income for the average local family. There was a lightness, a humour to the occasion which made the heavily armed P.L.A. contingent seem superfluous. This was the local people's day and they weren't going to allow outside influences to interefere with their enjoyment. Throughout the day the dragon boats raced back and forth across the river to the beat of drums, intermittent firecrackers and rockets. All this was to the accompaniment of loud Chinese and Dai music blaring out from tannoys. At the end of the afternoon the victorious crew, chanting and waving paddles aloft, danced to the stand to receive their trophy – an elaborate garland of paper flowers on a wire frame. They were to be seen prancing through the town for the rest of the evening in progressive states of joyful inebriation.

We visited the White Pagoda Park where cockfighting attracted huge crowds. Precariously perched spectators filled the surrounding trees, including young Buddhist novitiates in bright orange robes. 'Boys will be boys' seemed very apt. One might have thought they would be above such pastimes, or at least discouraged, but they obviously viewed the combat with relish. In the town's equivalent of an open air amusement arcade I even spotted a couple shooting pool, dark glasses, cigarettes dangling, consciously posing.

The actual water splashing was originally a more gentle affair, more in the nature of flicking and part of the courtship ritual. Whether it was the influence of the influx of foreigners I'm not sure, but the whole performance got a bit out of hand. We were not splashed, but drenched. Out on the street it was difficult to breathe when being assailed on all sides by buckets of filthy water from the city centre lake. The major object was to avoid getting a mouthful. However, good fortune is supposed to be relative to the amount of splashing you receive, and on this basis my karma seemed to be well assured.

The fortune of some of the Hong Kong students was not so good. They made the mistake of splashing the Public Security, wrongly assuming that they too would join in the carefree spirit of the day. Retaliation with truncheons was swift.

May 1st is of course a holiday in China. I had planned to extend this into a few days, fly to Chengdu, see Emeishan and Leshan and come back by train. All this was wildly over ambitious. By rearranging lessons and taking a mad dash in a taxi, costing half the 1000km railfare to Chengdu, I arrived at midday at Kunming airport. Having passed through

25

security, and so become a captive audience, we were then informed the flight was delayed until 6.30 p.m. A pleasant afternoon was spent reading and sunbathing on the balcony. At 7 p.m. we were told that the weather was poor and they wouldn't be flying. This is about par for the course. People have even been told that the plane couldn't take off because the runway was being cleaned. However patently absurd the excuse, this is always preferred to admitting that the plane has mechanical problems. In this case we had seen engineers working on the Chengdu plane all afternoon. Still there is no arguing with an airline, so we returned reluctantly to town. After a two hour battle at the airline office we finally extracted a refund. Not a very good start to our short break.

Next morning we got up early. By good fortune Helen, one of the Scots teachers, had previously given the ticket clerk at the bus station English lessons and through this excellent 'Guanxi' was able to get us tickets on the Dali bus. The journey takes eleven hours, give or take an hour or two for breakdowns and the level of the driver's mania. Before the construction of the Burma road it was a journey of 13 days. The road climbs first over the Western Hills and then twists and turns along the Kunming-Chengdu railway line, crossing backwards and forwards, while the line plunges in and out of an endless series of tunnels. Later on you pass through some incredibly rich farmland, intensively cultivated. Although this was only the 1st of May, the peasants were beginning to harvest the golden wheat. From the pass at the west end of this huge valley a magnificient view of greens, browns, yellows and gold stretched out along the valley floor as far as the eye could see.

Eighty percent of the population are the Bai minority or *min jia* of whom there are 1.1 million in Yunnan. The city has a long history, being the capital of the Nan Zhao kingdom from the 8th century when a local ruler defeated the Chinese army. It remained independent until 1252 when Dali was captured with much loss of life. Colonisation ensued, and after Kublai Khan overthrew the Southern Sung dynasty the whole of Yunnan was annexed under the new Yuan dynasty. It continued to be dominated by the Hui

(Chinese Moslems) until a major rebellion was put down, again with appalling loss of life, in 1874.

Dali sits at 6,000ft on the west shore of the Er Hai, a long and beautiful lake. The west and north sides are bounded by a line of 12,000ft peaks that hold a little snow right into May. The area has gushingly been described in tourist literature as the Switzerland of China. It certainly has the beauty, if not the facilities. The largest and most populous city in the area is in fact Xiaguan at the foot of the lake, an ugly industrial expanse of concrete. By comparison Dali has been left unspoilt.

Helen had been here earlier in the year and received a warm welcome at the Number 2 Guesthouse, so no argument about Chinese price accommodation. The next day we walked down to the lake, swam in the clear blue water, admired the picturesque fishing boats and wandered amongst the rice paddies. On the way we stopped at a new-looking temple. The villagers happily went for the key and showed us into a brand new gaudily painted hall. They informed us it had been constructed in the last year by donations from the three work units of Cai Cun village and had cost 10,000 yuan to build. As elsewhere in China where religion is important to minority groups, the party's attempt to destroy it has not ultimately succeeded. Although the physical manifestations, the temples, monasteries and shrines have been demolished, the spirit, the idea and the practice of devotion have remained.

The area around Dali is comparitively rich with fertile and productive land. The commitment of such a large sum of money after the strictures on religious observances had been relaxed is nonetheless significant and tells us a great deal about the people's priorities in life. This same morning we also had a look round a substantial new house that was being built for a local businessman, we were told for about 15,000 yuan.

Dali is dominated by three large pagodas, the San ta the main one leaning rather like the Tower of Pisa, this variation probably dating from the time that much of the city was destroyed by an earthquake. The pagodas themselves are largely undamaged, but many of the surrounding buildings have obviously been used as barracks and then vandalised, with graffiti everywhere.

On the second day I set off early to climb Cangsban (12,900ft). Although still dusk, loud music and incomprehensible exhortations blared forth from tannoys at an acommodation block. Soon though I had climbed out of the valley into a different world. For an hour I followed a track and accompanied three Bai hill people on their way to cut bamboo. The girls stopped occasionally to pick light pink rhododendron flowers, but I could not understand their attempted explanation of their purpose; I assumed medicinal, or perhaps it was simple joi de vivre. We parted at a small temple perched precariously on the hillside where an old lady opened up the hall to set the daily scene with joss-sticks and rice offering. I could have tarried longer in this idyllic setting with the morning sun that had risen over the Er Hai beginning to warm the air, but my goal lay beyond.

Pine forest gave way to dense bamboo thickets. I could hear the shouts of the bamboo cutters and occasionally one passed me heavily laden negotiating his way down the steep path. At the top of the thicket the path petered out into an entanglement of rhododendrons, in places almost vertical. This was more like tree-climbing than mountaineering, pulling myself up from branch to branch, constantly getting my small daypack entangled. At the upper reaches of the rhododendrons pockets of snow still lay on the ground. I climbed up into thick mist. The wind increased. I put on my anorak. It was cold. At last I reached a ridge, but was very soon disconcerted to discover that it was a real ridge similar to many I had scrambled on in the Scottish Highlands. But I was not prepared for this. My hands were frozen, my clothing inadequate. I had no map or compass, could hardly see where I was going, and would not necessarily know where I had got to when I got there. I was also beginning to be affected by the altitude. This was the highest I had ever climbed. Oh dear – that awful realisation that this was a bit foolish. Surely the summit must be somewhere. 'Ah', a sign of civilisation, a broken pipeline to follow, and in due course I arrived at reputedly the world's highest manned TV relay station; a stark concrete tower, surrounded by rusting iron girders, with a rubbish tip spreading down the hill – easy, a few steps from the front door and heave.

The station has a permanent crew of three. There were also a couple of photographers from China Railways on location, a bit disconsolate with about 20 yards visibility. They told me the view west was magnificient when you could see it. In the meantime they helped me thaw out with cups of tea and sticky buns. Over the next couple of hours a whole party, including children, appeared through the mist. They had taken two trucks up a track that led three-quarters of the way up the mountain and then followed a broad path to the summit. So much for scrambling on exposed ridges. One of the photographers, Wang, had about as much English as I had Chinese and we had an animated discussion on photography, which kept us entertained as I helped him carry his equipment down to the trucks. They had been on the summit for three days and decided they had enough shots. He informed me he was one of six photographers working for China Rail and was dispatched all over China.

From Dali they were going south over the mountains to Baoshan. It sounded like an attractive, very independent and, by Chinese standards, very well rewarded job. After a climb of over 6,000ft and a descent of a further 3,000 I was quite happy to accept a lift back down the track. Panoramic views of the evening sun breaking through the clouds highlighted selected spots in the mosaic around Dali and the lake.

An experience I missed because of my late return from the hill was the local line in massage. This could be obtained at a shower house, itself something of a rarity. The masseur was an old deaf-mute, the massage full body job including testicular squeezing. I suppose there's not much you can do if he's got you by the balls and appears immune to attempts at communication.

It is rumoured they intend to build an airport in the valley and if they do the whole character of Dali will alter dramatically. In the meantime the number of foreign devils is limited by the eleven hour bus ride which inhibits most tour groups. The instinct for development is, however, all too apparent. There is already a Peace cafe, a Coca Cola cafe, a Garden Restaurant.

Sadly our time was strictly limited. Two days in a bus for two days in Dali might seem excessive, but such was its charm that even this short visit was very well worth the journey. Peter Goullart, an emigre Russian employed by the Nationalist government, promoting co-operatives in Lijiang in the 1940's recalls of this route 'the prospect of travelling the Burma Road used to fill me with dread'. During the war years it was a notorious killer. I am happy to report that it is now no worse than most other roads in SouthWest China.

3

BACK ON THE ROAD
AGAIN

After three short months I left Kunming on a sticky grey midsummer's day, my first taste of China rail, following the route taken by the road to Dali that I had travelled in May. Towards evening the sky was clearing and we passed through some dramatic scenery with the solstice full moon reflected off the swift flowing upper reaches of the Yangtse. This and the country to the west, where the great rivers from the Tibetan plateau force their way down through the mountains in deep gorges within a few miles of each other, Yangtse, Mekong, Salween, Irrawaddy and a bit further west the Brahmaputra, is ideal country for 'Alph The Sacred River' to run through 'caverns measureless to man'. It is a wild border area where it is obvious why Yunnan was largely cut off from Sichuan. This is exemplified by the recently constructed railway line with its hundreds of bridges and tunnels. It is another impressive monument to Chinese engineering skill but entailed considerable loss of life of both 'volunteers' and forced labour.

To my surprise I appeared to be the only foreigner on the train. It had been rumoured that there would be great pressure for places as the line had recently been cut by landslides. Fortunately I found the experience of hard sleeper sufficiently bearable to consider facing future journeys by this mode of transport. The hard sleeper consists of a coach with an aisle down one side with small fold-down seats by the windows. Across the aisle are a series of six bunks, three on either side, perhaps 10 of these, sixty in all. The middle is recommended. On the top you bang your head on the ceiling and are liable to suffer from claustrophobia. On the bottom you will be joined by half the other occupants of the coach who, besides wanting to view the *Waiguoren* are looking for extra space to eat melons, toilet their children, etc. Most of these trains, the long-distance expresses, also have a dining car where the food is expensive for the very poor quality. Unless you have come sufficiently prepared with your own supplies you will have to depend on this or packets of junk food from platform vendors. The trains are pulled by diesels which do a good job through very difficult terrain. One complaint I did not have was lack of punctuality.

Alighting at Emeishan in Sichuan at 6.45 a.m. I took a three-wheeled pedicab to Emei town, a bus to Baguo and a minibus to Wannian. In the latter we were regaled with full volume Chinese cover versions of the Beatles classics 'Hey Jude' and 'Can't Buy Me Love', a somewhat incongruous start to ascending a holy Buddhist mountain. As the day progressed, and the extent of the commercialisation of Emei became apparent, this early morning experience no longer seemed so aberrant.

From Wannian it was over seven and a half hours of climbing to Jin Ding, the Golden Summit, at 9,700ft, where I enjoyed a good meal followed by a magnificent sunset. This was a rare treat given that the summit is shrouded in mist for all but a few days every year. Almost better than the sunset itself was the mad scramble for posed photographs with hand outstretched to cup the setting sun; clever use of flash to create modern Buddhist magic.

I managed to obtain a dormitory bed on the third floor of the summit temple. With fading maroon paint and creaky woodwork it still maintained an atmosphere that was distinctly lacking outside, which was a spreading encampment, part building site, part refugee camp. Maybe, because it is a long way to the summit, this temple had not suffered the damage that had been wrought on others lower down from the depredations of the Red Guards, though inaccessability does not appear to have deterred them elsewhere.

I was seriously misled about the expected time of sunrise and so froze for a couple of hours. I had at least staked out a good position. I hadn't anticipated I would have to jostle like a press photographer at a photocall to catch a mountaintop

1. Kunming backstreet.

2. Gold finial on Jokhang roof. Lhasa.

3. Young beggars in the Barkhor. Lhasa.

4. Roof courtyard in the Jokhang. Lhasa.

5. Bridge to Gomulingka. Lhasa.

6. Clockwise circumambulation of the Barkhor. Lhasa.

7. Gold centrepiece, roof of Jokhang. Lhasa.

8A. Triple image of Tsong Khapa at Ganden Monastery.

8B. 'Mao is out'. Roof of Ramoche. Lhasa.

sunrise. The sunrise was suitably impressive, but far surpassed by the setting moon on the other side with mountains stretching away to Tibet, including the mighty Gongga Shan, the ice mountain, steeped in glaciers. The saying goes, 'that to behold Gongga Shan is worth ten thousand years meditation'. If this is so then this morning was a quick step along the path to nirvana. Gazing out on this visual feast it didn't occur to me that I would be headed this way in just three weeks time.

The Emei climb is in fact thousands and thousands of steps, the tedium alleviated by noodle, tea and soft drink stalls every few feet of the way, with the occasional fine view out through the trees. Porters sweat their way up with sacks of coal and others carry rocks which seemed ridiculously sisyphian. Even little and large ladies, some not so old, are carried up by the same means. This struck me as a particularly bizarre manifestation of the new China, to have peasant porters transporting large Shanghai ladies on a Buddhist pilgrimage. I wouldn't have thought you would gain much merit from attaining the summit by this method.

For many, maybe the majority, it appeared to be an extended version of the Sunday outing to the nearest temple to consume ice cream, take photographs, distribute litter and deafen with your temple-blaster. To give some semblance of devotion, however, there were little old ladies clicking rosaries, burning joss-sticks and chanting mantras, black turbanned merry widows. Most impressive of all was a girl with no legs I passed on my descent from the summit who was pulling herself up with her hands from step to step.

After sunrise, before descending I made my way across to the true summit through head high thickets of bamboo. This was an idyllic spot, away from the crowds and commercialism at Jin Ding. Perched on a rock I marvelled at the lushly wooded green mountains with wisps of white cloud floating below me, a sight definitely worth coming a few thousand miles to see.

From Emei it's a two hour bus ride to Leshan. Arriving late in the afternoon it was hot and sticky, a distinct change in climate from either Yunnan or mountain-top Emei.

Tagging along with other pilgrims making the circuit I
obtained accommodation at a guesthouse for only 1.80 yuan,
the cheapest during my whole time in China; it was
immensely satisfying to get Chinese price and escape from
the officially sanctioned lodgings. Relieved of my rucksack I
took a ferry across the river to inspect *Da Fu* – the world's
biggest Buddha.

Begun in 712 A.D., the masterpiece of the monk Haitong,
he is carved in red sandstone out of the rock overlooking the
confluence of the Min and Dadu rivers. These were reputed
to be dangerous waters, and were made considerably less so
by the infill from the carvings. It is a strange sensation to
stand on his giant toenails even if, with growing vegetation,
they are badly in need of a manicure. Unwittingly I seemed
to have embarked on a tour of sights of Buddhist
significance.

Sadly I realised that if I was to make Kaifeng and catch my
cousin Liz before her intended date of departure that the
next part of the journey was going to be a race against the
clock, a self-imposed burden in relation to China travel, but
at the same time something of a challenge. Could I achieve
my goal and maintain my sanity at the same time? Success in
China travel is not guaranteed. If, however, you have no
deadlines to meet and do not mind going with the flow, or
becoming becalmed for a while, then a leisurely progress can
be made. On the other hand if your life depends on arriving
at a certain place at a certain time then you are likely to be
seriously disappointed.

I left Leshan again by bus. Not a good start to the day as I
discovered that I had lost another filling along with a large
chunk of tooth wall. Many hours were to be spent over the
next few days anxiously poking my tongue into the
impressive cavity anticipating what awful remedies might
have to be faced. I was still adjusting to the heat and
humidity. The bus journey was slow and uncomfortable
over miles of road-mending. In retrospect I could look back
on all this as a training exercise or toughening up process for
the rigours of real travelling in Tibet, but at the time it was
quite unpleasant enough. During the seven, rather than four,
hours as advertised the monotony of the journey was relieved

by falling into conversation with a Dutch couple. Funnily, after just a day away from all western contacts, these blonde nordic types at first seemed very foreign and strange. I am dark haired and brown eyed and in the more far flung parts of the Chinese Empire have been mistaken for a member of the Han race. This was more so after the effects of Tibetan high altitude sun and a few weeks of encrusted grime had disguised my pallid western skin. The bright light also helps to screw up your eyes in the manner so diplomatically referred to by the Duke of Edinburgh as 'slitty'.

I remained in Chengdu two nights, just long enough to obtain a hard sleeper ticket to Chongqing where I arrived at 4.50 a.m. and boarded a bus for the Chaotianmen booking office at the other end of town. The aisles of the bus were full of brown emaciated coolies in ragged clothing carrying bundles on poles so heavy they could hardly get off the bus. Besides the bus, which at least put me into this century, I could have been in another age.

At Chaotianmen I started in the wrong queue. Fortunately I realised my error before too long and then only had to queue for a further four hours. When I was just two from the front of the queue (only 4th class left at this stage), I was grabbed by a scout from a shipping company and almost forcibly removed to a cafe to book a 3rd class birth for the following day. I was happy enough to get the birth, but bitterly resented the 5 yuan booking charge after waiting so long in the queue. No doubt if I had not been so keen and had turned up at 9 a.m. I could have got the same ticket without queuing at all. On the other hand I would not have had the opportunity to observe early morning life in the huge booking hall. A crackly 'Auld Lang Syne', a great Chinese favourite, on loudspeakers at 6 a.m. was probably an experience I could have done without.

Chongqing I was only able to afford one night on my whistle stop central China tour, leaving on one of the fleet of modern Yangtse steamers at 8 a.m. in pouring rain. The weather remained the same for the next two days. Third class is an eight birth cabin. Fourth class has twelve. Fifth class is camping out on the deck. In egalitarian China there is no first class. For this read second. Boating down the

35

Yangtse is a very relaxed and pleasant way to travel. The pace was unhurried and I was able to sit in the cabin at a desk and catch up with some correspondence. The scenery was unremarkable, besides some fine examples of riverside pollution. Sadly, in their rush to modernise, the Chinese are making all the same ecological mistakes that we started making right from the beginning of the Industrial Revolution. Having gained all the economic advantages at the time, however, it hardly seems reasonable for us to take the high moral position now.

That evening we docked at WanXian a provincial city of about 1 million close to the border with HuBei. From what little I could see of the city in the dark and the rain, it is near vertical, built up the steep Yangtse banks. On leaving the boat we had first to cross a pontoon of logs before climbing up a series of steep steps through an archway onto the main market street. The sensation was like entering some medieval town with rich and unpleasant odours and glimpses through crude windows into primitive sleeping quarters.

On the main street was a hive of tourist related private enterprise, in this case directed mainly at the Chinese tourists themselves. A trip down the Yangtse is a lifetime's ambition for many, and with the increasing wealth and greater freedom of movement the boats are now always packed. Goods on sale included cane furniture and rush mats for which WanXian is noted. Also on sale, and I was assured a local delicacy, were a whole range of pig extremities with the hairy bits still on; tail, nose, ears, trotters and some other bits I did not care to identify. For once I felt like a true tourist retiring from this exotic but squalid scene to spend a comfortable night on board.

Not long after getting under way again at dawn we entered the first of the three gorges (SanXia) for which the river is justly famous. In fact the river banks never properly level out again until you emerge from the last of these. The gorges are all equally impressive with extraordinary vertical rock faces rising hundreds of feet out of the river. The currents are swift and dangerous, the scale dwarfing our not inconsiderable steamer. Worcester, in his fascinating

36

descriptions of river navigation in 'The Junkman Smiles' goes into the details of how, before the days of steam power, junks were drawn up by trackers from rapid to rapid, a complex system of ropes being employed to steer past the innumberable eddies and semi-submerged rocks. The river rises and falls up to 50 feet when in spate, a massive volume of water being channelled through the gorges. The Chinese summarise their attitude to the problem in the saying 'it is more difficult to ascend to Sichuan than to ascend to heaven'.

Immediately after passing through the massive Gezhouba dam the boat docked at Yichang. It has long been regarded as the gateway to the upper Yangtse and was an important walled city as early as the Sui dynasty (581–618). In 1887 it was opened up to foreign trade by the Chefoo treaty concession forced on China by the British. During my few hours in town I saw no sign of this. I made directly by bus for the station and after a little flirtation with the ticket girl, a new experience after four months in China, bought a ticket to Luoyang, having been assured there was no direct way through to Kaifeng. The pace of life had definitely slowed down. Such leisurely ticket buying would be unthinkable in Sichuan.

Six hours overnight hard seat and I set off again from Xiangfan at 11.30 a.m. on what turned out to be the Chengdu-Shanghai express. I had to fight just to get on the train and spent the next eleven hours sitting bunched up on the floor. Hot, sticky, surrounded by highpitched jabbering, sick children and the accumulated detritus of a couple of days of close quarters living, this method of travel, although cheap and not too slow, is an experience only masochists would want to repeat. At least if you have done it once you can swap horror stories with future fellow travellers. To get out of the coach I literally had to climb over a mountain of bodies. There was no water left on the train and the only remedy was to pass money out to buy beer from platform vendors. The theory was that not only would this be thirst quenching, but I might even get slightly anaesthetised. One positive aspect of this kind of journey was that I had plenty of time to study Chinese both culturally and linguistically.

Otherwise the journey outside the train was unremarkable. We arrived in Kaifeng at 9.43 p.m. on 29th June just eight days after I left Kunming.

The experience of travelling on my own, and at least for some of the way well off the main tourist route, was a rewarding one. Although my language was limited there is nothing like repeating your story to dozens of inquisitive Chinese for confirming what you do know. I had also been exposed to several different regional dialects which had helped improve my ear for the unexpected. I was now about to be confronted with *Kaifeng hua*. Kaifeng, unlike most other urban centres has grown little in the last century, the population now standing at 300,000. This belies the fact that at one time it was the capital of the Northern Song dynasty (960-1127). Occupied by the Japanese during the Second World War, both the university campus and the neighbouring 11th century Iron Pagoda were extensively damaged. Many valuable books from the library were burnt for fuel during the cold winters.

Kaifeng impressed as more backward and less sophisticated than the South. With the exception of its famed melons *xigua*, the food is on the whole poor and uninteresting. Local delicacies are steamed bread and boiled cabbage with fatty pork. Henan is a poor province, for although it is central and fairly fertile, it has been fought over almost continuously and suffered a series of devastating floods. The Yellow River *(Huang He)* is less than an hour's bike ride north of town. Many times over the centuries it has burst its banks, or changed direction. The loss of life and livelihood has been appalling. In 1939 the retreating Nationalist Army blew up the dykes in order to halt the Japanese advance. The result was about a million Chinese drowned, hardly a move to improve this regime's shaky support.

For the four days that I was in Kaifeng it was hot (up to 36°c) and very humid. Visibility was poor. Life inside was only rendered bearable by the constant use of fans. Mosquito attacks were a great irritation and caused me to errupt like a plague victim. This coupled with a heavy cold, the first since I had been in China, and probably picked up on the train, gave Henan a very different complexion to Yunnan. I could now see why Liz had expressed some degree of jealousy about my walking into a teaching job in Kunming.

Getting to know her, however, more than amply made up for any deficiencies in the climate. We had hardly seen each other in ten years besides briefly at weddings or funerals, but because of a shared experience of character-forming Borders holidays during our childhood we didn't have to go through the preliminaries of relationship building. Liz's isolated situation in Kaifeng and my arrival from a different kind of China experience, coupled with having spoken no words for several days but Chinese, was for both of us most conducive to non-stop conversation.

One reason for Liz's comparitive isolation in Kaifeng was that the majority of the teachers were very definitely in the missionary mould and there appeared to be a trade developing with conversions for potential college places in the U.S. a particularly invidious form of 'rice Christianity'. Although the government's return to some degree of religious toleration is commendable, it seems strange that they should be prepared to tolerate the obvious implied interference in domestic affairs that this barely disguised missionary activity entails. Cynically it has been noted that on the whole these teachers are easier to recruit and can be paid much lower wages. A rather dubious saving I thought.

When it was known that I was travelling to Beijing I was allocated a lecturer from the university to help me on my way. Although well intentioned, my previous experiences of allowing others to organise my travel arrangements had not been happy ones. As time ran out we were forced into a mad rush by bus to the station but didn't arrive in time for my companion's 8 p.m. lecture. Nonetheless he insisted on escorting me to the Beijing train and attempting to help me get a hard sleeper. He appeared to think escorting a foreigner was more important than a late lecture and I could do nothing to dissuade him. In the event the train was packed and even tracking down the chief ticket inspector *(che zhang)* failed to produce a sleeper – another crowded, hot, dirty and uncomfortable overnight hard seat ride. With four whole days to prepare in Kaifeng you would have thought I would have learnt my lesson by now. So immediately after finding suitable accomodation in Beijing, and chastened by my overnight experience, I set off to book a plane ticket.

Before leaving Kunming I had been paid two months salary in 5 yuan RMB notes. These cannot be taken out of the country and such a large wad rather spoilt the cut of my moneybelt which had not been designed with this in mind. I had therefore decided for both time and comfort to fly the next part of the journey. In the event it turned out that over the next ten days there were no seats available on the few flights to Lanzhou and Xining, so on impulse I bought a ticket back to Chengdu instead.

I had by this stage decided to go west. In any case the Russian Embassy was not handing out any visas for a month, and taking a train ride past Chernobyl so soon after the reactor disaster did not seem like a good idea.

I had come to Beijing primarily to get a Pakistani visa to cross over from Kashgar. When I phoned the embassy I was assured that the problems on the border had now been resolved and that there was definitely no need for a British national to obtain one. Given the fickle nature of these arrangements, I would have been much happier with a piece of official paper.

From the airline office I went to look for Wang, the photographer I had met on the top of Cang Shan above Dali. After a little searching down the *hutongs* (alleys) I found his office and made an arrangement to meet the following day. He also most generously provided some slide films from their film safe, a better guarantee of quality than other films I had so far been able to get hold of.

My second day in Beijing I spent with Wang doing the sights including the Forbidden City *(Gu Gong)*, the Temple of Heaven *(Tian Tan)* and the North Sea Lake *(Bei Hai)*.

In the late afternoon we abandoned sightseeing and returned to his flat. This, set in an old courtyard near the centre of town, was the most opulent and westernised I had so far encountered; stereo, colour T.V., carpeting, his own framed cibachrome prints on the walls. I had hardly recovered from the gastronomic excesses at lunch time before being bombarded with an endless stream of jiaozi (steamed meat buns) and other delights that his wife produced from a small kitchen across the alley. She was employed in a secretarial job and their joint standard of living was by local standards quite high. By preferring not to have children they also reaped the rewards of extra allowances and good housing.

De rigeur is a visit to the Great Wall which is suitably thought provoking. It comes as no surprise that the foot of the wall is entirely devoted to tourist souvenirs. The Chinese have a saying that 'if you haven't mounted the Great Wall, you haven't visited China', so now I had both 'mounted' and 'visited'.

From Beijing I flew back down to Chengdu. I had by now become almost blasé about air travel in China. Sitting next to a Chinese computer engineer on her way to instal new equipment in Sichuan, I was able to reassure her that flying wasn't as terrifying as she had thought. On the other hand, of course, she might know something about internal flights that I did not. My recall of the brief period I spent in Chengdu for the second time might best be summed up as life in China sometimes seems like an endless round of eat, travel, eat, visit temple, eat ad infinitum, or nauseam.

41

4

THE FORBIDDEN CITY

"You might find yourself in
another country, and you might ask
yourself how did I get here?"
Talking Heads

For thirty years since the Chinese invasion in 1950 Tibet once again became a forbidden kingdom. In 1979 a few favoured 'foreign friends' came first, followed by a trickle of intrepid travellers and then the floodgates opened to tour groups. By 1986 special travel permits were no longer necessary and official avenues of exit and entry had been established. There were flights from Chengdu, and buses from Golmud in Qinghai to the north and Katmandu in Nepal to the south. All routes led to Lhasa. Rioting in 1987 led to a reimpositon of restrictions and it may be that 1986 was the last real opportunity for a while to travel off the officially sanctioned corridors. Conversely and ironically the imposition of martial law in Lhasa may encourage travel to the less accessible parts, and there will always be a few who will delight in finding the hardest and most adventurous routes through closed areas.

On a grey muggy morning I left Chengdu in an ancient Russian jet for the two hour flight to Lhasa. Even with my Chinese ID reduction this is one of the most expensive internal flights, but considering the untold hardships early explorers experienced, the majority of whom never got anywhere near Lhasa, a simple flight seemed very much like cheating.

It was overcast on takeoff, so Gongga Shan, the ice giant I had seen from Emeishan, was sadly invisible. After an hour, in compensation, the extraordinary panorama of the Himalayas came into view, an incomparable sight from such a vantage point. Laid out below us like a vast exquisitely fashioned relief map were rows and rows of huge peaks, covered in snow, glistening in the sunshine.

On landing the first things to strike me were the unusual quality of the light and the thinness of the air. It is this more than anything else that sets Tibet apart from anywhere else I have ever visited. For the next five weeks I was not to drop below 11,000 feet. The snowline in summer starts between 17,000 and 19,000 feet. Most of the central plateau lies at 14,000 to 15,000 feet, so although several of the world's larger mountains are in this area they don't exactly tower over you. Particularly in treeless West Tibet the scenery is surprisingly not unlike parts of the Scottish Western Highlands, especially the Highlands in early spring with the old snow hugging the mountain tops in a barren and desolate landscape.

It is over an hour's bus ride from the airport to Lhasa which gives plenty of time for the adrenalin to build up in anticipation of finally arriving. Alternatively you can sit choking in the dust, wondering whether you are coming down with altitude sickness. Besides obvious considerations for siting the airport well out of town, like a sufficiency of flat ground, superstition may also have played a part. They are not after all likely to be too concerned yet about urban sprawl or the environmental lobby. When the Dalai Lama was in residence, he lived right at the top of the Potala, the magnificent hilltop palace, in order that no mere mortals should look down on his holiness. Overflying was therefore understandably strictly taboo. An American aircrew that got lost in a storm flying the 'hump' in 1943 flew over the city before crashing into a hillside. This must have afforded immense pleasure to the monks who had prophesied that any persons attempting such sacrilege would instantly be struck down. In truth the siting of the airport probably has more to do with Han strategic considerations, keeping their lines of communication well away from threats from the local population.

The first impression of Lhasa is how different it is from other Chinese towns. One might simply argue because it is not Chinese. Although there is an equally large new concrete

Han city it is the old Lhasa with its dirty alleyways, gaily decorated windows, door designs and hangings that is quite rightly the soul of the place.

Set at almost 12,000 feet, Lhasa now has a population in the region of 60,000. Over half of these are Han Chinese, and it is clearly a garrison town, utilitarian concrete surrounding the ancient Tibetan heart of the nation. It is dominated by the massive Potala with its white walls and rooftops gleaming with gold. Just to the west of this is Chokpori, one of Tibet's four holy mountains and the former site of Mendzekhang, the famed medical school, until it was destroyed during the fighting of 1959, to be replaced by a T.V. aerial. Whereas the Chinese are busily pursuing this perceived modernisation, there has been a resurgence of interest in traditional medicine in the West. At its foot a few monastic buildings are now being rebuilt. This is in line with the new policy in Tibet in which it is now admitted that there were 'excesses', in most other people's language 'outrages', and some effort has been put into presenting a more acceptable face to the outside world. The desirability of this, however, is not agreed by the conservative powers in Beijing. Hu Yaobang's removal from office in 1987 was partially thought to have been for inadvisably expressing regret about Chinese 'misrule' in Tibet.

This acceptable face entails a modicum of reconstruction at a few carefully chosen sights, primarily of touristic interest. During the worst 'excesses' much of Lhasa was torn down, but Tibetan Buddhism with its cycles of rebirth is ideally suited to absorbing and reconstructing. As mud bricks are the principle building materials the old quarter appears rapidly to have reverted to its former state. Edmund Candler, the Daily Mail correspondent who reached Lhasa with the Younghusband expedition in 1904 commented, 'Lhasa, like the Tibetans, is very dirty.' He described it thus: 'We found the city squalid and filthy beyond description, undrained, unpaved. Not a single house looked clean or cared for. The streets after rain are nothing but pools of stagnant water frequented by pigs and dogs searching for refuse.' Much of the city is very little different today.

One of the surprising aspects of Tibetan life was that

although Buddhism has been the all important focal point, they were quite prepared to tolerate the practice of other religions, as long as there was no attempt to convert Tibetans. Down a side street at the far end of the Barkhor, the central pilgrim concourse, a mosque is still in daily use. This has for many years catered for the religious needs of the small community of Muslim traders that have resided in Lhasa. Muslims have also filled the role of butchers. As Buddhists the Tibetans are reluctant to take life, although many are not averse to eating meat, so the Muslims presence perhaps neatly evaded this tricky issue for them. Clearly this made life easier than getting animals to strangle themselves which was occasionally used as an alternative method. Outside the fertile Tsangpo valley, and certainly for the nomads on the Chang Tang, life without resorting to eating yak and sheep would be insupportable.

The city has not always been forbidden and when the borders were closed this was primarily aimed at non-Asians. Pilgrims, in particular from the neighbouring states, have always been able to move about with some degree of freedom, in much greater danger from bandits and robbers than from the central authority.

If not exactly cosmopolitan, like all capital cities it too has had its fair share of outsiders in residence. The most celebrated of the Westerners was Heinrich Harrer who became tutor to the fourteenth Dalai Lama, Tenzin Gyatso. Harrer and Aufschnaiter, two Austrians, were climbing in the Himalayas when the Second World War broke out and they had the misfortune to be interned by the British authorities in India. They succeeded in their second escape bid, slipping across the border into Tibet. After many adventures and over a year of travelling, mainly on foot, they arrived ragged, half-starved and penniless in Lhasa. For a while it was touch and go whether they would be allowed to stay or whether they would be handed back to the British. Aufschnaiter, an engineer, busied himself with irrigation schemes, but it was Harrer who became a household name in the West through his excellent autobiography 'Seven Years In Tibet'.

From the bus station I made my way down the half mile of

the main street to the Banak Shol Hotel, where I was somewhat disconcerted to receive my first lesson that the ability to communicate in Chinese was not universally welcomed or respected. Unfortunately a new edict had just been issued increasing the minimum hotel charge to 10 yuan – nothing like having a captive clientele. After a couple of days I managed to transfer to the Beijing East Tribal Hostelry, which was run by Tibetans and appeared to be defying the authorities by only charging 6 yuan. ('Tribal' I thought a rather surprising translation for *'Minzu'* ; more usually taken as 'minority' though its clientele both Tibetan and traveller gave it a wild air for which this was an appropriate adage.) As long as you could get a room at the far end from the toilets, which from here on became progressively less savoury, it was if anything more comfortable than the grander Banak Shol. On the other hand it lacked a direct view of the Potala from the toilet block, surely the most magnificent of settings to match the sublime with the mundane.

The first evening in town I met two of the travellers whose company I had shared on the top of Emei Shan. We enjoyed some fine river fish at the Darkay Restaurant while they regaled me with their exploits on a seventeen day truck ride through East Tibet. This was not bad timing for this difficult route. The area is slashed by numerous deep river valleys and the roads, such as there are, are frequently cut, particularly at this time of year when some of the monsoon rain gets through. They had had the very good fortune to fall in with a survey crew equipped with jeeps and all the necessary supplies. Not only had they travelled in relative comfort, but had also been exceptionally well fed. Their other two companions had not been so fortunate, and did not arrive in Lhasa for another four days.

My attempt to view the sights of Lhasa got off to a poor start with both the Potala and the Norbulingka, the Dalai Lama's former Summer palace, closed. At least at the bus station I was able to find out about buses to Shigatze. The main bus station is well out of the centre of town, a vast completely empty hall, very different to bus stations in China. Because of this absence of people, however, it was by far the cleanest I came across and in stark contrast to the filth and squalor for which Tibet is famous. Outside is a large liberation monument, Tibetan on one side, Chinese on the other. A 'liberation' monument can hardly seem in good taste to the majority of Tibetans and, maybe conscious of this fact, the Chinese have chosen to erect it well out of town with the P.L.A. garrison in between.

On the way back down the Lingkor, the five mile outer pilgrim circuit that surrounds the city, I passed a couple of yak skin coracles, the traditional method of river crossing still in daily use, then made my way across the small suspension bridge, decked with hundreds of prayer flags, onto Gomulingka Island. These prayer flags are predominantly about a foot square and have either texts, mandalas or images of Buddhas stamped on them. Their production assumes the proportions of a major industry at the monasteries. The huge numbers placed at every conceivable strategic spot is living proof of the unbowed faith of the Tibetans. This mass of gay colours flapping gently in the breeze sets off nicely the blue sky, bare earth and rocky hillsides. In almost any other climate they would quickly rot. Here they only appear first to fade then tear later in the wind. The Tibetan, *lung-p'ar* (wind pictures), seems most apt.

This 'Island of Thieves' is a popular spot for Lhasa citizens, who come particularly on Sundays to picnic, play and wash clothes in the river. Some of the braver ones even go swimming in the near freezing water. Down near the river, by coincidence, I bumped into the English teaching fraternity and was invited to join them for a picnic lunch. This included local delicacies like small new potatoes and chang. *Chang* is a form of Tibetan beer. As a homebrewer the closest I have come to it before is barley wine about two weeks into the fermentation process. Whether from its own natural potency or whether it is the altitude, it is certainly effective.

Teaching is a small world in China and so it was no surprise that here in Lhasa were teachers who had mutual acquaintances. On my way back into the old part of town, as if deliberately to confirm this observation, I ran into Dave from Kunming, who had finished teaching a week or so after me and then set off directly for Tibet. It was Dave and his travelling companion, Rebecca, a doctor from Newcastle, who introduced me to the Beijing East Tribal Hostelry.

Together we repaired to the Banak Shol for dinner. At the time it had a bad reputation for subsequent digestive disorders, but tracking down the source of any such infections is a pretty hopeless task when surrounded by such low standards everywhere. The alternative is to give up eating out altogether, as several of the travellers opted to do and simply eat out of tins. But this is no long term solution if you anticipate staying in Tibet for more than a few days.

At the Banak Shol you choose your own food and, for the ultimate in diner's participation, maybe even cook it yourself as well. Prices for a bowlful are arbitrary, but not unreasonable. Here I sampled my first yak which had a slightly gamey taste, though it might just have been a little high. The most entertaining spectacle, not for the squeamish, was one of the kitchen girls cutting up yak meat with a long handled axe, a task she carried out with considerable enthusiasm. Rebecca was visibly horrified by the lack of hygiene, but then having travelled in from Katmandu, she had not had the benefit of a few weeks acclimatisation in China, which if not so extreme still wins no hygiene awards.

After this interesting feast we went to visit the two teachers who had set up a travellers co-op based at the Banak Shol. This useful enterprise provided information, books on loan, even camping equipment, which made sorties out into the countryside possible for many who had travelled in from the hotter parts of China and were unprepared for the rigours of the rather different Tibetan climate. Unfortunately the organisation also seemed to attract the sort of objectional travel know-alls whose only role in life appears to be putting down other travellers by making them feel less experienced. This seemed a very puerile attitude to travelling.

I had, I now think, rather naively expected that the majority of people that I would meet on the road would be fascinating, worldly wise and sympathetic characters.

Although the friendships one makes is for me one of the prime reasons for travel it is also sadly my experience that travellers are not all, per se, wonderful people. Indeed I was surprised to find that the get up and go required to reach outlandish places is not in itself a recommendation. Is it physical travel itself that opens up our eyes? We can also travel in our heads, in our dreams. This can be done both at home and on the road, but for me the stimulus of real, rather than imagined, new worlds lead to an activation of the latter and an awakening awareness.

The teachers had just moved into a top floor flat in a large old town house. The flat was at the far side of a courtyard looking out through a big bay window at the substantial gateway. This would have formerly been the residence of one of the Tibetan nobility and was situated just a little way back from the Barkhor. This was a very much more romantic place to live than in one of the more modern Chinese buildings in the separate Chinese part of the city. It was at their flat that I first sampled tsampa (barley flour), usually added to tea. On first acquaintance I was not overly enthusiastic, and I rightly suspected that adding it to rancid yak butter tea was going to be no improvement at all.

The following day I rented a bicycle from the Kirey Hotel and set off to ride out to Drepung monastery, but before I had gone very far it became obvious that the bike was faulty. What was supposed to be an easy way to travel thus turned out to be a major feat of endurance. Besides prolonging the ride out by going too far and being rerouted back round a P.L.A. camp, I had to drag the bike almost all of the way back again. By this stage both the brakes had ripped off and the back wheel had seized solid. Under any circumstances dragging a bike on its front wheel three or four miles is no fun, but I was conscious of the fact that I was not yet fully acclimatised, and the last thing I wanted to do was incapacitate myself on the second day.

Much has been written on the subject of altitude sickness, its symptoms, effects and treatment. What is not clear though is why it is so selective. Some very high risk categories, like overweight geriatrics with heart conditions manage to fly in and out without undue problems. Some fit young climbers who have previously had successful Alpine seasons get very seriously ill as soon as they get over 15,000 feet in the Himalayas. As preparation spending a few months in Kunming at 6,000 feet would not have done me any harm, though some people have even suffered from altitude sickness flying there. In the event I got back into town rather breathless, but was probably from more danger if high blood pressure from my apoplectic outburst at the bicycle hirer than I was from the effects of altitude. (Must remember, count to ten, adopt attitude of extreme patience, exercise compassion.)

Drepung monstery, founded in 1416 used to be the world's largest with 10,000 monks. It was a separate town in its own right and one of the most powerful institutions in the country. Some fierce fighting took place round about during the uprising and the monastery was later ransacked. With charred buildings and broken flagstones, destruction is still much in evidence. Today there are 400 monks and novices who have been allowed to return by the Bureau of Religious Affairs, who effectively control numbers. Religious freedom as so far reintroduced is only limited. At Drepung though, something of the old spirit lives on. The main chanting hall, the *Tsug-gyeng* is complete and in daily use. In the massive kitchens butter and tsampa sculpture was being prepared to be placed on the shrines as *'torma'* – holy food. From the roof of the *Tsug-gyeng*, with bright sunlight shining on its gold finials, there were rich views of the Potala dominating Lhasa, green fields of barley, a multiplicity of shades on the surrounding hills.

We next planned to go to Ganden, but it rained all night and it did not seem such a good plan at 6.30 a.m., so I went back to the Jokhang, the central cathedral, instead. It was packed with pilgrims, this being one of the few days when the major shrines were all open. The crush of people waiting patiently in line, the smell of yak butter lamps, the hazy lighting, the eerie religious objects encrusted in centuries of grime, the murmur of many mantras a steady drone, imparted an element of mysticism more than sufficient to impress a western sceptic and clearly just what the eager pilgrims had travelled so far to experience. Sadly Lt. Colonel Waddell expressed the general view of the British occupying forces in 1904 when he descibed the Tibetan 'holy of holy's' as, 'this revolting and bizarre spectacle of barbaric idolatry'. At the back of the building is a partially covered courtyard containing on three sides large gilded prayer wheels, their wooden handles worn smooth by the touch of countless pilgrims. My prayer-wheel spinning career started in fun and inquisitiveness at the Jokhang. It soon became a compulsion. Was it a religious insurance policy, which couldn't do me any harm, or was it the elusive search for perpetual motion?

The Jokhang is the most important religious building in Tibet, the religious heart of the nation. During the Cultural Revolution it was taken over and turned into the Red Guards No. 5 Guesthouse, complete with the Han's favourite meal, the pig. This was all part of trying to undermine and discredit the Tibetan's religion. They certainly couldn't have acted more provocatively or with less taste than this. Work is now being undertaken to repair some of the damage. The crowds of pilgrims appearing daily, some even making full-length prostrations around the Barkhor, suggest that the attempt to destroy religion has failed. Exact figures are uncertain, but the monasteries have maybe been reduced from 1,600 to 20. But what is certain is that where they have tentatively come back into existence they no longer have any control over secular affairs. The spirit of religion, however, is fundamental to the Tibetan's way of life. Although their monasteries have been destroyed, the monks degraded, disgraced, killed or dispersed to labour camps, the communist cadres have not been able to stop the people from daily observances that are as much a part of their way of life as sleeping or eating. Particularly among the older people prayer-wheels are turned, juniper is burned to send the spirits heavenwards, prayerflags are erected on mountain tops and passes, *'0 mane padme hum'*, Behold the Jewel in the Lotus, is endlessly repeated. This is not a society that has lost its religion.

The Barkhor and its adjoining streets house Lhasa's main Tibetan markets. Pilgrims and traders, often one and the same, come from all over the country to make clockwise circumambulations. For the most part only travellers and foreigners, the occupying Han Chinese, ignore this religious custom. Bicycles are not so much in evidence, reflecting the relative lack of affluence. Large character signs in Chinese and Tibetan hang overhead forbidding riding round the Barkhor.

Before 1950 Tibet was effectively a pre-money economy, and barter is still an essential element in most business. Goods range from the exotic, Buddhist antique statuary, semi-precious stones, Khampa knives, even a snow leopard pelt, through the food section with a poverty of vegetables but plenty of yak and sheep gore which is overlaid with the pervasive smell of rancid yak butter and cheese, to incense, prayer flags and juniper. Thus a whole section of the market caters for devotional practices.

From the Jokhang I went on to the Potala, a day on which many sections turned out to be closed. I did wonder, though, what lay beyond all those doors, leading, it is recorded, to over a thousand rooms. Were great splendours being kept from view, or were the doors closed because most of the contents had been carted off to Beijing? Certainly this has been the fate of innumerable objects looted from Tibet. Such looting calls into question the Han Chinese view of their 'conquest' of Tibet. If Tibet were truly a part of Greater China then looting your own territory seems somewhat incongruous and illogical.

From the roof by the Dalai Lama's former quarters you can look down on the city and imagine him as a young boy scanning the people below with his telescope intent on discovering how they lived. The building itself is one of the most extraordinary in the world and it is fortunate that it, at least, was spared serious structural damage during the troubled times that Tibet has known in recent years. It is suggested this was only because of the direct intervention of

China's then Prime Minister, Zhou Enlai.

To make a day of it I returned via the Ramoche, Lhasa's second temple. Originally this housed princess Wen Cheng's Sakyamuni Buddha that was brought from Chang'an in the seventh century. Sakyamuni, 'the ascetic of the Sakyas', was reputedly born into the Sakya clan, minor nobility in the Nepalese Himalayas, and this appears to be corroborated historically by a commemorative pillar discovered in 1895 and attributed to the Emperor Asoka, dated 249 B.C. This was some two hundred years after Sakyamuni's birth when the Buddha tradition was no doubt still very much alive. Sakyamuni went on to become the young Siddhartha, metamorphosed in time through complete renunciation into Gautama.

King Songtsen Gampo (608–650) was the young warrior king who unified all Tibet and made Lhasa his capital. He married two princesses, one Chinese and one Nepalese, and they jointly converted him to Buddhism. Princess Tritsun brought a smaller Sakyamuni from Nepal and this originally was housed in the Jokhang. At some stage the two were swapped over. Waddell further displays his prejudices when he describes the Chinese Sakyamuni, by then in the Jokhang. 'So inferior is it to anything I have seen in China,' he writes, 'and so unlike in feature any type of Buddha's image there, that I doubt the story of its foreign origin.' There is, however, no doubt about the veneration in which the Tibetans hold it, whatever its origins. The Ramoche was gutted in the 1960's and its treasures looted. Recently half the smaller Sakyamuni was found in a rubbish pit in Lhasa; the other half was saved from being melted down for scrap metal in Beijing. The two halves have now been reunited back in the Ramoche. On the roof I was amused to find a sign of the times. Mao is out. A pile of metal backed portraits of 'the great helmsman' had been crumpled up and thrown out, great idols cast down; an eye for an eye.

I had started taking Tibetan lessons along with David and Rebecca from the Banak Shol manager. He spoke quite good English, having spent some time studying in India. This was a great start into the language, as the phonetic systems applied to the language have not made pronunciation at all easy for beginners. Tibetan also has many honorific forms which almost constitute a separate language, so it is necessary to distinguish what is actually in everyday use. Obviously as with Chinese, honorific forms are less common than they used to be. It is interesting to note though, that as *'tongzhi'* (comrade) has to some extent gone out of vogue in China, some of the older forms are coming back in. Maybe the same will happen with Tibetan. Having said that, there are also many different dialects in Tibetan which further complicate the issue. With regard to the use of *'tongzhi'* Dave was berated in Kunming for addressing a Chinese lady in this manner. "You have no right to call me tongzhi, you're a foreigner", thus precluding or dismissing the possibility that a foreigner might be a member of a Communist Party sharing some of the same aspirations. From being a general form of address in China, it now tends more to be used exclusively by members of the same club, danwei, or cadre.

Dave, who taught linguistics, found a book in Chinese explaining the phonetics of Tibetan. I also bought a copy. It only cost 25p. The extreme pretension of having this slim volume on my bookshelf will sadly be missed by all but those conversant with Chinese and Tibetan. Unfortunately such a reference work has an extremely limited use outside China, and few Chinese have shown any enthusiasm for learning what they regard as a language of barbarians.

As in Xinjiang a major weapon in the Sinification program has been the control of access to education. Without Chinese, progress into the party cadres, and therefore upward mobility in this far from classless society, is virtually impossible. In 1987 Tibetan was declared once again to be the official language, though how real a change this was intended to be is open to question. There is only one Tibetan University and little or no educational infrastructure other than Chinese schools for the children of Han colonists and administrators.

During the Cultural Revolution it is doubtful whether any Tibetans received any other language teaching than Chinese. In Kunming I was shown an extraordinary experimental textbook *(shi yong keben)* produced in 1970 at the Technical

College *(Gong xueyuan)*, at that stage a hotbed of Red Guard activity. It starts with Lesson One: 'Long live Chairman Mao'. Presumably a good starting point should you have found anyone else in China brave or foolish enough to be talking English at the time. Lesson Two: 'Karl Marx', and so it progresses until Lesson Eight: 'Long live Mao Tse Tung thought', when the alphabet is introduced. It continues in this vein until Lesson 22: 'What is this? This is a tank. What is this? This is an atom bomb. (These both illustrated). But the best weapon is Mao Tse Tung thought.' (Not illustrated).

At last in Lesson 23 we see a portrait of English life: 'Jenny is a poor English girl. She has three wishes in her life. First she wishes to have a Chairman Mao badge. Second she wishes to have of copy of the Quotations of Chairman Mao Tse Tung. Third she wishes to go to China and see Chairman Mao with her own eyes.'

In the final lesson the purpose of this study is revealed. Lesson 24: 'We study English for the world revolution. We'll use it to propagate invincible Mao Tse Tung thought to struggle against imperialism, revisionism and all reactionaries.' Maybe the Tibetans were fortunate enough to have been spared this kind of nonsense – in English at least.

I often thought back to class days in Kunming and wondered how the eager young pioneers at YunDa would have viewed the forcible suppression of the Tibetans. Would they make the leap in logic encouraged in the official line that they must have been bad elements or counter-revolutionaries, or would they simply be in a separate category of 'barbarians' requiring civilisation? Their attitude to the treatment of 'criminals' was revealing. Competition for my attention during English lessons came mainly from the ringroad. As a continual backdrop to the days teaching, changes in the noise level were quickly noted. With the whole south wall window, I enjoyed a panoramic and frequently distracting view of life below. On more than one occasion a fleet of motorcycle outriders and sidecars roared up the road flashing blue lights and hooting sirens.

These would be followed by a couple of trucks of

prisoners, heads bowed in submission, facing out for the people to stare at, between each prisoner an armed guard. Such a sight was an excuse for the whole class to rush to the window, following the example set by their teacher. I asked where the prisoners were going, the deadpan reply, 'maybe they transfer prisons, maybe they are shot'. This they took for granted as only natural and just. Obviously capital punishment, always a good debating subject, was a non-starter here. The idea of taking a non-party line, for the sake of debate had not yet caught on.

In Tibet I saw no wall poster displays of convicted criminals as I had in several cities in the east, Kunming, Chengdu, Kaifeng. Black and white photographs and character text protected from defacement behind glass civic notice boards graphically detail criminal activities and the resultant penalties, frequently execution. Such dehumanised and depersonalised images I regret made little impact on me. I was too far removed from the reality that was their tragedy. Perhaps in Tibet they had simply abandoned all pretense of exerting this kind of subtle pressure. Luo Zhang qi in' Half of Man is Woman' refers through the mouth of the piebald horse philosopher to the fact that they are living in 'unprecentedly ridiculous times'. Perversely he sees life in the Chinese gulag as the only sane place in the topsy-turvy Chinese world. In Tibet a strong tradition already exists of an alternative value system in which the search for freedom from desire is ranked on a different plane from the more mundane considerations of the pursuit of power, wealth and status. The occupying forces have an insuperable task, for the Tibetans appear to be playing a completely different game.

A posting to Tibet has long been regarded by the Han Chinese as a form of punishment. I certainly cannot recall meeting any who expressed great enthusiasm for being there. Historically most of the Ambans who were sent out to represent the Chinese imperial authority were cashiered or reduced in rank for fraud or embezzlement. Thomas Manning, the eccentric oriental scholar who reached Lhasa in 1811 commented 'it is very bad policy thus perpetually to send men of bad character to govern Tibet'. The same might be said about General Rong, the Red Guard leader, who was removed from office in 1980. Whether he was personally responsible for many of the excesses, or simply failed to check them, his period in power was a particularly unhappy one for all concerned.

Through a contact in Kunming we were given a surprising address to visit in Lhasa, that of an official artist and his wife. Fortunately for my untrained ear she spoke beautifully clear Putonghua. This might in part have been because through her work as a CITS guide she was well used to contact with foreigners. Unfortunately the light was very poor in their flat as it poured with rain all evening, and Lhasa was suffering a blackout. What I could see of his work, however, I very much liked; a cross between Tibetan images and surrealism. As a Hui (Chinese Muslim) he held an unusual sense of the contradiction between his admiration for the Tibetan spiritual heritage and the destructive force of the Cultural Revolution.

Outside Lhasa sky burials take place almost daily. Only the very rich or important citizens could afford alternatives in a country where fuel is at a premium and the ground is frozen for much of the year. The Tibetans' solution is to dismember the corpse, pound up the bones, and feed the remains to the vultures. A process that seems well in tune with the Buddhist belief in the insignificance of the body and its emphasis on cycles of rebirth. We were shown some very gory photographs of sky burials he had taken, which confirmed my opinion that this form of voyeurism was not an essential part of my Tibetan itinerary. This was not because of the distressing process of disposal of the dead, which I regard as rather more tasteful than some of the sanitised methods in the West, but because this is surely a private and a family affair. The negative attitude of the Tibetans to onlookers, Chinese as much as Westerners, is hardly surprising. Would you like a busload of Tibetans turning up at the village church to photograph your mother's funeral?

The rain slackened off during the night, so we slipped out early from our lodgings and made our way through the silent streets to the Barkhor to wait for transport to Ganden. The

Barkhor is very eerie at 7 a.m. when it is still dark and quite cold even in July. The occasional passerby, mainly stooped and elderly, added juniper to the stupa shaped hearth. This constitutes an offering and bestows blessing. It is a most evocative and romantic smell, for me the quintessential essence of Tibet, and one that when I next come across it will transport me instantly back to this very scene. Juniper is one of the few plants that grows with any ease in this very harsh climate. Since they do not appear to make gin, this seems as good a use for it as any. Much energy goes into gathering, drying and transporting the plant, an activity with very limited economic significance and a classic example of the Tibetan sense of priorities.

Ganden was founded by Tsong Khapa (1357–1419) Tibet's great reformer and founder of the yellow hat sect, the Gelug-pas, who have retained ascendency over the older red hat sect since. It is situated 45 miles east of Lhasa at 14,000 feet in a natural amphitheatre. Up until 1959 it had 4000 monks and was the third most important monastery, after Drepung and Sera. During the uprising in 1959 the monks offered considerable resistance, some of them belonging to a warrior sect. They were only finally subdued after the P.L.A. shelled the monastery. The buildings were then systematically blown up and further Red Guard vandalism took place in the '60's. Two major chanting halls have now been rebuilt by volunteer labour and others will follow. The scene, however, is still one of utter desolation. I was told that about two hundred monks had returned, although without permission, but I did not see evidence of nearly so many. The monks we met here were particularly friendly and keen to show us all that was being rebuilt. For once I was positively encouraged to photograph images of their founder Tsong Khapa; a photographic triumph, hand held, yak butter lamp lighting. Tsong Khapa invariably comes with a large central figure flanked by two smaller identical versions on either side. The statues most notable features are severe and piercing eyes below peaked pixie hats.

In the main hall we were treated (if that is the term) to yak butter tea with tsampa. The idea is to roll the flour in the tea through the fingers of one hand to make a compact ball. My attempt was a disaster with the dough clinging to my fingers. Obviously more practice is required to become efficient at one handed kneading. My discomfort might have been lessened if at this stage I had come to realise the Tibetans innate sense of amusement and ability to laugh at minor absurdities. If tsampa was all I had to live on and its availability infrequent and not guaranteed I might have treated this offer with greater respect. I made what I thought was an impressive performance of getting it down without too much grimacing. Dave fared rather less well.

On the roof two craftsmen were fashioning new hands for Buddhas, in a little production line. They were certainly not old enough to have learnt their trade before the monastery was sacked, so this was a newly acquired skill. They appeared surreal in Mao hats and tunics, clutching slightly larger than life sized hands.

Further up the hill I caught an eerie playing of *geleng* and *dong*. The geleng is a version of the reed blown *shawn* or *suona*, the dong is like a massive Alpenhorn and makes to my ear a rather unmusical noise like a fog horn. It seemed, however, particularly appropriate to this mournful setting, bellowing out over the valley below. An old monk was instructing two apprentices, so that the old skills should not die out.

From there I climbed on round to the top of the hill several hundred feet above the monastery following a couple of young Tibetan women who were carrying bundles of juniper. They made a most romantic sight tending the juniper fires and attaching prayer flags to the mountain top poles. At the highest point there were three dogs waiting, like guardian spirits or monkish reincarnations. Possibly they are attracted here as a site for sky burials, but their presence at the time seemed more like an extension of the supernatural. Tibet, though, is full of the mystical and they did not seem greatly out of place.

Ganden is one of the saddest, but perhaps most fitting monuments to the meeting of the old Tibet with the newly regained Chinese Communist, dare one still say Imperial, authority. Lost cities hold a sense of history, of loss and the passage of time, but it is very difficult to come to terms with such a magnificent monastic city having so recently been deliberately and completely destroyed. Cities have been sacked, fired, abandoned, but only in this century do we appear to have perfected the means of wholescale obliteration.

5

THE BATTLEFIELD TRAIL

On the 17th July we set off early to get the Shigatze bus, passing on the way a squad of P.L.A. soldiers jogging down the street. On reaching the traffic island a girl dropped off the back to spit, while several others decided to break ranks for a quick rest and rejoin the squad on the way back. We had prime position at the front of the bus, but in order to take possession we had to evict a German, disguised as a pixie in a red anorak, clutching a cine camera. My values were obviously beginning to change, as I felt no qualms or pangs of conscience about this, indeed more a warm glow of satisfaction at a job well done. Survival of the fittest mentality had set in.

Throughout the ten hour journey it poured with rain and in several places the track was near impassable. At the bridge over the Brahmaputra (Tsangpo) south of Lhasa the metalled surface ended. There was to be no more, besides a few central streets in Shigatse, until just south of Ye Cheng almost 2,000 miles west in Xinjiang. At times the bus driver seemed to have lost touch with the road, if not with reality. En route we passed first over the Khamba La pass at 15,274 feet, the traditional boundary between Front and Back Tibet, *U* and *Tsang*. Piled on the summit were numerous cairns of *mane* stones with prayer flags fluttering in the breeze. Even with poor visibility the views were dramatic on both sides. To the south we looked down on the Yundrok Tso, a huge turquoise lake in the shape of a giant scorpion, the third largest in Tibet. It is reported to be full of primitive scaleless fish, a form of carp, which Waddell grandly names *'Gymnocypris Waddelli'*. On the other side of the lake, the road climbs up again to cross the Karo La pass at 16,548 feet. This was the site of the highest recorded battle in military history. Ghurka and Pathan troops climbed to over 19,000 feet in order to attack the Tibetan positions from above. This campaign, one of the least edifying in British Imperial history requires some amplification.

From the seventh to the ninth century, Tibet was a small but strong military power and carried out devastating raids into both India and China. The most notable of these invasions led to the capture and brief occupation of the Tang Imperial capital at Chang'an in 763. It has not always been a case of 'presents from China, tribute from Tibet', as Chinese histories would generally have us believe. During the Yuan Dynasty in the thirteenth century, the age of the Great Khans, the rise of Lamaist Buddhism became an important factor in the regional politics of central Asia. Tibet has enjoyed periods of unification and effective independence, as in the reign of Tsong-Khapa in the early fifteenth century, but has also suffered from external interventions often related to the succession of the Dalai Lamas. These came both from the Mongols, who sacked Lhasa in 1717 and from invasion by the Manchu Imperial forces during the seventeenth and eighteenth centuries. By 1750 the Dalai Lama ruled through a council of four ministers, the Khablons, but was deemed to be under the supervision, more or less, of the Chinese resident, the Amban, who was supported by a garrison of 1500 troops. In the last century of the Ch'ing dynasty China was being torn apart by the Opium War and the Taiping and Boxer rebellions and consequently had little energy left to exercise effective control in Tibet.

British contact had been made with the Tibetans as early as Bogle's mission to the Tashi Lama in 1774. He is credited, on Warren Hasting's advice, with introducing the potato to Tibet. He was followed by Captain Samuel Turner's expedition eight years later. Neither, however, had managed to get further than Shigatze and contact had not been made with the Dalai Lama and the Lhasa authorities. Subsequent attempts proved no more successful. The Sikkim Convention in 1890 signalled the internationalisation of the Tibetan problem. The problem was clearly by external definition. Britain failed to force Tibet to open its borders despite its aggressive mercantilist policies.

Lord Curzon has been regarded by many as perhaps India's greatest Viceroy. He was certainly not lacking in vision or drive, but he appears to have elevated the 'Great Game' with Russia to an extent where a forward defensive policy was carried to an extreme. He bitterly attacked all 'those who decry British interference anywhere and extol the odious theory of sedentary and culpable inaction'. He is quoted in 1899 as saying, 'whatever be Russia's designs on India, whether they be serious and inimical or imaginary and fantastic, I hold that the first duty of English statesmen is to render any hostile intentions futile'. In the light of subsequent events one might be forgiven for asking who was responsible for the fantasy. On the other hand it is easy for us in hindsight to question the whole sorry enterprise, but the problems certainly appeared real at the time. We probably underestimate the importance of prestige, which was the fragile force, rather than the force of arms, that bound the border states of Nepal, Sikkim and Bhutan to the rule of the British Empire. All these three it should be noted were originally part of Greater Tibet.

At the end of the 19th century Tibet appeared to be a political vacuum. Although China claimed suzerainty, it was clear as their empire crumbled that they exercised no real control at all. The assumption was that this vacuum must inevitably be filled and that, if the British did not do something, the Russians most certainly would. After all they had been eating up central Asia at a rate of 50 square miles a day for the last couple of decades. The bogey of Cossacks pouring through the Himalayan passes into India's soft underbelly was for the British quite a real fear and, in terms of Russia's long term goals, not an entirely unrealistic prospect. In many ways movement into the North-West of India would have been a great deal easier for the Russians than a thousand mile advance over Tibet's inhospitable terrain. Control of Tibet itself was not regarded as a prize that would justify the immense effort that would be required to secure it.

Curzon believed it was essential for the British to establish some form of relationship with the Tibetans. Consequently he sent two letters to the Dalai Lama. Both of these were returned unopened and Curzon chose to take this as a deliberate slight. There was no indication that these letters ever reached the Dalai Lama. At this stage the mysterious Dorjieff played his critical role in the development. In 1900 and 1901 this Mongolian monk from Sera Monastery turned up in Moscow bearing letters from the Dalai Lama. The British were furious, as they had recently been informed he never wrote to foreign governments. To cut a very confused story short, these fears, both real and imagined, engineered border incidents (mainly to do with boundary markers and yak grazing), and Curzon forcing the pace in opposition to Balfour's Conservative Government that was weak and in disarray, led to the dispatch of a mission into Tibet. Candler justified this by claiming, 'we were drawn into the vortex of war against our will by the folly and obstinacy of the Tibetans'.

From the outset the division of responsibility between the diplomatic mission, headed by Colonel Younghusband, and the forces commanded by Brigadier MacDonald, was not clear. Brigadier MacDonald seemed an odd choice. During the Boxer Rebellion he had held the unusual post of Director of Balloons, which hardly suggests he was regarded as an outstanding officer. Throughout the campaign he was criticised for overcaution and came to be known as 'Retiring Mac'. Younghusband, a protege of Curzon, was the complete opposite. It was against this background that the battle at Karo La took place. There had already been a slaughter of the hopelessly outgunned Tibetan forces at Guru. Beseiged at Gyantse, Younghusband deliberately chose to ignore, until too late, a telegram from MacDonald not to advance. Colonel Brander, the senior officer at Gyantse was praised for most effectually carrying out 'his object of removing threats to our line of communication'. This is a strange way of describing an action 47 miles in advance of their position. Although in no way diminishing the bravery or daring of the action, it does perhaps indicate the superiority they both felt and enjoyed, that they should have advanced to attack a force of over 3,000 dug in at 16,000 feet with only 400 soldiers. Such confidence did, however,

9. Drogpa shepherdess at hot springs. Coquen.

10. An offering of juniper incense above Ganden.

11. Ganden Monastery. Founded 1417 – destroyed 1960's.

12. Dong and Geleng practice. Ganden.

13. New hands for Buddhas. Ganden.

14. Gyangtse main street after the monsoon.

15. Prayer-wheel wall on pilgrim circuit. Shigatze.

16. Horses at Chang Tang truckstop.

turn out to be justified by a resounding victory, leaving the way open to Lhasa.

When the force did finally push on to the capital, the Dalai Lama had fled and there was no sign whatsoever of any Russian involvement. The treaty that Younghusband negotiated was largely repudiated by his own government and he was censured for being overzealous. The Earl of Roseberry sarcastically alluded to what he saw as the 'desire and ambition of the Indian Government to impose the drinking of Indian tea on a people which preferred Chinese tea.' Such, perhaps, are the strange ways of Tibet that Younghusband experienced a revelation on a hilltop above Lhasa and subsequently devoted his considerable talents to founding the World Congress of Faiths, in an attempt to bring different religions closer together.

In the long term the most notable result of the expedition was that by reaching Lhasa and then withdrawing, the British created just the vacuum they were originally trying to avoid. The Chinese historian Tieh-tseng Li commented on the Manchu Amban in Lhasa, Yu-T'ai, that 'he proposed to avail himself of the British occupation as a means of asserting Chinese authority over Tibet', indicating the weakness of the Chinese position at the time. Britain's failure to enforce the original terms of Younghusband's treaty requirements lead the Tibetans to believe yet again that they were very much stronger than they actually were, and wholly unprepared for the Chinese invasion when it finally came in 1950.

The Lhasa Convention of 1906 was inconclusive and had no Chinese or Manchu signatories. In 1910 Chao Er-fang, the new Chinese Amban attempted to reassert control and this lead directly to the flight of the thirteenth Dalai Lama. The following year, however, Chao was murdered and the Chinese Revolution threw the country into turmoil. The last Chinese troops left in 1913, evacuated through India, the Dalai Lama returned, and Tibet was left very much to its own devices for the next three decades. The Simla Tripartite Conference broke up in 1914 with no further progress on the question of Tibet's status, other than the drawing of the McMahon Line which was to have consequences later on in border disputes between China and India. The thirteenth Dalai Lama died in 1933 and the Panchen Lama in 1937. For a brief period there was a move back to a pro-Chinese stance under the Regent , Ra-dreng, but he in turn was ousted by the more pro-British Young Tibet group. From the early 1930's China was in any case largely preoccupied with Japanese encroachment and Communist opposition.

From the Communists point of view, certainly immediately post liberation in 1949, the idea of extending the virtues of their particular interpretation of Marxism/Leninism beyond their existing borders had taken on almost the status of a crusade. They had just defeated the Nationalists on the mainland were well organised and determined. They broadcast that their next intention was to liberate Taiwan, Hainan and Tibet. They were soon to be at war in Korea. They pursued the establishment of Chinese backed Communist parties throughout S.E.Asia. They were exporting their ideas to the West and to Africa; in essence world revolution. In Tibet in their eyes not only were they consolidating their western defensive frontier, but they were doing the Tibetans a favour by delivering them from the oppressive yoke of foreign influence, principally British, and the greed and cruelty of their rulers, both religious and secular. In an attempt to pursue the former they went to great lengths to produce evidence which was as thin on the ground as the British presence and probably accounts for the particularly harsh time in imprisonment suffered by Robert Ford a British radio operator working for the Lhasa government who was captured near Chamdo during the first few days of the PLA invasion in 1950 and was not to be released until after the end of the Korean War.

In taking this stand over Tibet the Chinese Communists have in fact maintained consistency with the position of both Chinese Imperial and Nationalist authorities before them. Right up to 1949 and Chiang Kai-shek's hasty retreat to Taiwan his government in all discussions continued to state adamantly that the question of Tibet was an internal affair.

In October 1950 the PLA advanced on Chamdo in East Tibet. The Tibetans didn't even inform the outside world until several weeks after the invasion had begun. The message to the Chinese and other foreign powers appeared to be that the Tibetans were far from serious in their determination to resist. In fact some of the regular Tibetan troops and Khampa levies fought with distinct bravery, but unfortunately lacked organisation, leadership, and any overall strategy. Nonetheless, Tibetans have born the British little illwill for our indifference in their hour of greatest need. In the context of Britain's shattered morale in the Far East after the Second World War, our reluctance to get embroiled in a problem that few knew or cared about is hardly surprising.

Since there had been remarkably little diplomatic activity or lobbying to establish Tibetan independence in the international eye, it was a foregone conclusion that Chinese claims that Tibet was an internal problem would receive tacit acceptance. India, having inherited the mantle of British policy, and Britain itself, to their joint shame, ignored the moral principle at stake and effectively did nothing.

Historically the Dalai Lamas have been both spiritual and temporal leaders. The spiritual element has been regarded as the more important. One in three Dalai Lama incarnations have died in childhood during periods of regency. A regency has always been in the interest of the Chinese, as a Dalai Lama in power can provide a rallying point for Tibetan nationalist aspirations. It is widely suspected the Chinese had a hand in many of these deaths. It is for similar reasons that they fear the return of the present Dalai Lama. On one level this would suit their purposes admirably, by bestowing some degree of legitimacy on the current status quo, but they have demanded that the prime pre-requisite of a return would be a renunciation of, or at very least an agreement not to pursue, any question of Tibetan independence. However, any such acknowledgement would itself undermine much of the authority that he would possess with his people. The Panchen Lama was effectively a Chinese puppet, kept in Beijing with a notional position of authority as head of the Bureau for Buddhist Affairs. His stock in Tibet was not very high, until he was surprisingly allowed to make a speech from the Jokhang on a visit back to the country. Contrary to the Chinese expectations, he repudiated much of what had happened since the uprising and was quickly hustled off back into effective captivity. As a result though, he did his standing with the Tibetan people no harm at all.

There is sadly an insensitivity on the part of the Han Chinese which even after thirty years means that there has been little real integration. In part this is the historical arrogance which has treated the Tibetans, as it has other Minority groups, as little other than backward and barbaric and thus requiring the supposed civilising influence of Han Chinese cultural superiority. Tieh-Tseng Li in 'Tibet, Today and Yesterday', whilst claiming impartiality, betrays this bias in such statements as Tibetan histories are 'histories of a religion rather than chronicles of a people', ignoring the fact that for most Tibetans the two were inseparable. It could be argued the Tibetans have as much right as any other national group to interpret what is their history for themselves. He indulges a tendency to dismiss or diminish the basis of Tibetan culture in such remarks as 'eventually Tibetan bloodthirstiness was converted into a passion for spiritual satisfaction', as if the latter were merely an extension of the former. From the Tibetans point of view practically everythin that has happened to their country in recent years has been a deliberate attempt to destroy not only the people and their will to resist, but all that they hold dear in their way of life.

When the Dalai Lama fled in 1959 with 80,000 of his followers it was not immediately realised what a complete disaster was about to overtake the country. The Chinese now admit some mistakes were made. This is something of an understatement. It is estimated that anything up to one in seven lost their lives. Monks previously made up one in five of the male population. You do not see very many today. Whatever deficiencies the old Tibetan society had, and these were admitted by the Dalai Lama, who was keen to introduce some reforms to drag the country into the twentieth century, it was not common for there to be shortages of food. It was a hard, and in the remoter parts, lawless society, but the hardships were for the most part attributable to the extremely harsh climate.

The Chinese tried to get the Tibetans to grow wheat, preferred by their own home market, to barley, the traditional Tibetan staple crop. The wheat harvest failed and there was widespread starvation. It is perfectly clear that the ten years of the Cultural Revolution were a complete and unqualified disaster for the whole of China. This is publicly acknowledged in the change of leadership and policies, but privately a great deal more is said, and none of it is favourable. In Tibet the combination of Red Guard zeal and Han chauvinism lead to the worst possible excesses. It is hardly surprising that, albeit with some CIA backing, there was an effective guerilla army operating out of Mustang in inaccessible North-West Nepal right up to the 1970's. They were only finally defeated and tricked into laying down their arms when the Chinese and Nepalese forces combined to leave them no further avenue for manoeuvre. By this stage some had been fighting for twenty years.

Ultimately the question must be by what right does one ethnic group impose its rule, both political, economic and cultural, on another distinct and separate group in an identifiable geographical area against the expressed wishes of the latter and where they have occupied that space for a considerable length of time. Jonathan Mirsky, the Observer correspondent, has likened the Tibetans struggle to that of the Palestinians against the Israelis in the occupied West Bank, in effect their own *Intifada*. This is a particularly embarrassing comparison for the Chinese to stomach as they have for long been critical of Israel and supporters of the PLO.

It would clearly be attractive to adopt the Dalai Lama's overview and see the Chinese invasion and subsequent occupation and repression as a matter of limited significance in terms of the overall history and unfolding of the Buddhist path. His position of moral ascendancy is unassailable, the Nobel Peace Prize simply recognition of this. For many young Tibetans, even given their immense respect for their spiritual leader, I suspect this offers little comfort. The Dalai Lama has been marginalised in their hatred of their oppressors. Exercising compassion can't be easy when your suffering has such a clearly attributable external source.

69

That Tibet has for too long been a pawn in world politics is undeniable and the manoeuvering of several governments, British, Indian, Russian, Chinese, have on the whole been a squalid and unedifying spectacle. Whatever historians may conclude about the historical status of Tibet, this is surely of less significance than the right of the Tibetans to self-determination today. China's plan is clearly to render this latter argument academic by moving rapidly towards a position in which the Tibetans are a minority.

My students in Kunming took it for granted that XiZang (Tibet) was an integral part of China and just another province in their vast country, albeit a remote and backward one. *Xizang* means western granary, (to be plundered perhaps), but *zang*, not inappropriately, can also mean dirty. They hadn't the faintest idea why anyone should actually want to go there. This just confirmed their view about the eccentricity of foreigners. For them it held the status of a Chinese Van Diemen's land. On that basis I was a remittance man.

On the run down from the Karo La the road follows miles of mud brick telegraph poles. These were constructed by the British in 1904. The story goes that monks at the time asked what they were for and were wisely told that the British forces wanted to be sure of being able to find their way back home. Taking this as an indication that they would soon be on their way, no attempt was made to destroy them. In this treeless wilderness the obvious building material was used and they have lasted remarkably well. Less successful were the transport arrangements. They suffered a fearful toll in pack animals, partly from the high altitude and harsh weather conditions, but primarily from lack of fodder. The report on the 'Supply and Transport Arrangements in the late Tibet Mission Force' notes that only mules were dependable. Even the hardy yaks suffered 80% casualties, although maybe most of them were eaten. On the table of pack animal casualties there is also an entry for coolies, used 10,901, casualties 88 = 0.87 percent. Native life was cheap even on your own side.

With David and Rebecca I had originally intended to go on to Shigatze, but the monsoon forced a stopover in Gyangtse. Anyway we had had enough bus for one day. The Gyangtse Hotel offered the basic amenities. My bed had to be removed from under a steady drip coming through the flat mud roof, but fortunately the monsoon rains only get through for a few days each year. Despite the inconvenience, I was glad to have witnessed its effect. There were to be quite enough bone dry days later on.

The hotel had a tearoom attached where you could make your own selection in the kitchen. Given our extremely limited command of Tibetan, self service was essential. The staples were *momo*, a yak equivalent of *jiaozi*, and a spicy potato dish. Potato is one of the main crops in central Tibet and was a welcome addition to the menu. This washed down with a few mugs of sweet milk tea (non-yak variety) made for a filling dinner. Adequate food supplies are by no means universal the further west you go. My memories are of long periods with what seemed to be nothing but the occasional bowl of noodles, interspersed with gluttonous excesses to re-stock, rather on the camel principle.

The next morning we went down to have a quick look at the monastery and arranged what we thought smugly was a truck to ourselves through to Shigatse. When we collected our luggage and returned to the truck, however, it had about twenty foreigners on board. Before we even got out of town, the traffic police appeared and a long argument ensued. According to the police a truck had crashed the day before and four people had been killed. Had a similar fate befallen twenty foreigners, who should not have been travelling by truck anyway and if it could be proved that they had let them leave town in such adverse conditions, then they might well have been held responsible. However, about half the occupants of the truck spoke some Chinese. Teaching staff from all over China seemed to have converged on Tibet at the same time and were trying to get to places the authorities did not want them to be. I sometimes wondered why there was this much tolerance. Opening the border with Nepal to individual travellers has lead to a great influx from the Katmandu 'scene'. This brings a lot of problems and very little in the way of benefits. Expensive, closely controlled tour groups are both very much more manageable and more lucrative.

To prove the point, the police were eventually beaten down by intransigence after everybody had had their say. The last laugh for the day, however, was for the police. They followed us out of town to where the main bridge was down after a night of torrential rain. There were wonderful scenes of chaos as more and more lorries drove into the river only to get stuck, strung out like an amphibious convoy for a couple of hundred yards downstream. It was obvious we were not going to get across and we returned to Gyangtse and a mad rush back to our respective hotels to ensure a bed for the night.

Towards evening the rain cleared and I went with Rebecca and Dave to have another look at the Kumbum. This magnificient building was constructed in 1427, and is reckoned to be the finest outstanding example of Newari art (Nepalese from the Katmandu valley). They are apparently still much in demand for their skill as craftsmen. It is constructed as a huge circular chorten, crowned with gold, which sits on a mandala shaped base, four stories high. On each level are a series of chambers, large enough to house life-size images of Bodhisattvas. Fortunately it was not substantially damaged although many of the surrounding Palkhor monastery buildings were razed to the ground. Founded in 1365 it housed 1,000 monks. A few are now in residence, but the atmosphere is not a happy one.

Gyangtse was the third most important city in Tibet, but it ceased to be a main centre of trade with the departure of the British agent in 1949. Above the city towers an impressive fort (*dzong*), which was left undefended when the British mission arrived. In order to cause less offence and also because of inadequate water supplies, they decided not to occupy it. The Tibetans appeared to be completely indifferent to the accumulated filth of generations. A party who had occupied a fort on the way up from the Chumbi Valley had spent the first few weeks there removing loads of rubbish in order to make it habitable. This may have influenced the decision not to occupy the fort at Gyangtse.

In the event it was a serious military mistake as the Tibetans reoccupied it and were able to fire down on the British camp below. Fortunately for them this was more of a nuisance than a danger as both the Tibetans' muskets and cannons *(Jingals)* were of limited range and accuracy. It did mean, however, that in due course the fort had to be retaken. Even with the limited artillery at their disposal, they were able to blast a hole in the wall, and once Lieutenant Grant of the 8th Gurkhas had fought his way in through the breach the opposition evaporated.

Like so many other strategically important buildings it was razed by the Chinese. Inside we found our way into a small burnt temple, where charred beams lay at jagged angles to the open sky. The walls were covered with the remains of barely decipherable painted images. It was unclear whether the blackness was the black skull cruncher, the grime of centuries, or the result of burning. From the highest point there were panoramic views down onto the muddy houses of the city below and out over the fertile plain with rich greens and yellows from ripening mustard. The plain is bisected by the swift flowing Niang river channelled in a straight line northwest to join the Tsangpo.

On the way down we made a circuit of the back streets, ankle deep in mud and the accumulated refuse from the neighbouring houses. Several of these had swastikas both clockwise and anti-clockwise, indicating that the animistic Bon faith, that was largely absorbed into Tibetan Buddhism, is still a living force in some quarters. It's reversed swastika is usually taken to be a reversal of time, to be against the natural order of things, associated with evil, the black arts, a destructive force. But then absorbed religions have never enjoyed good favour, as with the attribution of witchcraft and worse to pre-Christian rituals.

The rain had stopped the next morning, although much of the town was still awash. The main street, which the day before had been almost deserted, was now bustling with traders. This was to be an epic day. Much was to happen before we finally reached Shigatze at eleven at night.

At first we debated changing course and heading for YaDong to the south near the Sikkimese border. Three

73

foreign teachers from Chengdu were trying to get there, but couldn't make up their minds whether to accept a lift from five particularly wild looking Khampas. China may be a very safe place for women to travel unaccompanied. In Tibet there may not even be safety in numbers. Marco Polo speaking of the Tibetans, by whom he meant the Khampas, claimed 'the natives are idolaters and out and out bad'. This view appeared to be shared by the Lhasa Government who warned the British Trade Agent at Gyangtse in 1905 that they could not be responsible for the conduct of the Khampas, 'the people of Kham being evil persons'. This did not deter them, however, from using Khampa levies as a major component of the Tibetan forces and their fighting spirit and bravery was clearly recognised.

Rumours of border incidents with Sikkim abounded, although no one was sure of their source, so instead we set off to the Lhasa side of town to check out the vehicle parks. At the bus park we found an ancient bus and a truck full of pilgrims. It is apparently not uncommon for several families to band together to hire transport to combine business with pleasure and to have a holiday into the bargain. What I found most surprising was that there were some Han Chinese among the party. At first our supplications fell on deaf ears, but after we had shared some biscuits, tea and cigarettes, if not exactly inviting us, they did not forcibly remove us when we clambered on-board the back of the bus. Every available space was occupied, including metal chairs being parked all the way down the aisle, so getting on at all was quite an achievement. Our elation at this coup was shortlived, for the bus then proceeded to lumber down the high street to stop at the Kumbum. We were informed they were going to stop for a couple of hours to look round. At least this time we succeeded in getting into the Kumbum. It was then decided that the bus couldn't carry all the passengers (this seemed reasonable in view of the meal it had made of a few hundred yards along level ground) and we were now going to transfer to a truck. We then drove back up the street to our hotel to stop for lunch; four hours and back to square one.

At last we were off, but just around the corner an overloaded blue truck had bogged up to the axle and a particularly inept and incompetent job was made of extricating it, so we had to wait for another hour. At the river all was still chaos, so it was wisely decided to go and visit Naini Monastery in the other direction instead. This fortified monastery was also stormed by the British on 25th June 1904. They blew huge holes in the high defensive mud walls, which appear never to have been repaired, unless they were similarly breached by the Chinese. Much of the despoiliation, however, was certainly of more recent origin. Healthy crops in the surrounding fields were not reflected in the drawn faces of the settlement; a mutilated beggar at the gate, thin children, sullen and suspicious adults. Behind the monastery a sheer cliff rose almost 2,000ft, with the remains of a smaller fort on the summit outlined against a dazzling deep blue sky. About a third of the way up religious inscriptions were carved into the rock, too inaccesssible perhaps for even the most zealous of Red Guards to have destroyed.

On the return journey the ice had been broken and a party spirit prevailed with an exchange of sunflower seeds, sweets, nuts and raisins. A monastery visit invariably seemed to lift and lighten the mood. Despite the hardships they endure, Tibetan pilgrims appear to carry with them an irrepressible capacity for fun and laughter.

Driving back we discovered there was an alternative route along the riverside that was quite passable, but unfortunately the way was blocked by a road official, who was making the most of his sudden elevation to a position of unparallelled authority. He was initially unmoved by either the pilgrims ' entreaties or Dave's questioning his commitment to socialism. This latter exchange I particularly enjoyed, although I am sure tactically it was a mistake. In the meantime a couple of official and tourist landcruisers were allowed through. Rebecca had a deadline to make in Katmandu, and was becoming increasingly anxious. Her approach to one of these landcruisers met a complete stone wall. Any spirit of co-operation that there might have been between foreigners on the road seemed to be something of the past. There was also a very real divide between first and second class travellers. The degredation, if that is what it was, was progressive. By the time I reached West Tibet I was quite prepared to take any transport going and make any compromises necessary to obtain it.

Noting this loophole in the road block we transferred to a Chinese jeep. The principal passenger turned out to be a translator for the Panchen Lama who had spent several years at Dharmsala (home of the Dalai Lama in exile) and spoke reasonable English. After further argument we were allowed through. This was not to be exclusive. The official having had his moment of obstructive glory ordered the roadblock demolished and all the vehicles passed through. We then immediately broke down, so the advantage we thought we had gained in respect of accommodation was lost.

Before long we were off again, but after an hour stopped at the driver's village for a welcome cup of tea. This was the first Tibetan house I had entered. I would have liked to have photographed their impressive loom, but it was indicated that photography would not be welcome. When we finally arrived at the Tiensin Hotel in Shigatze we were treated like royalty and it was obvious that our jeep host was a man with a position of some importance in the Tibetan community, although he appeared to have no authority with the Chinese. In this sense there is very much a society within a society. This royal treatment even extended to being made a meal at midnight by the manager's family, a singular honour as they did not normally cook at the hotel. The most memorable aspect though, was being brought a bowl of warm water to bathe my feet, hospitality of a new and different order.

6

SHIGATZE

Although most of the residents were foreigners, the Tiensin Hotel retained a Tibetan atmosphere, with blue and black geometric designs on white canvas awnings and brightly painted door and window frames. There seemed to be more residents than there were rooms, but this just meant people sleeping out on the upper courtyard.

Shigatze had become a traffic bottleneck. The only way to get to Nepal is to travel direct from Lhasa. This normally involves an overnight stop in Shigatze, but there was a lot of competition for this transport, and prices were beginning to spiral upwards. An increasing number were travelling first to Shigatze in the hope of picking up onwards transport there. The result was that every bus coming into town was besieged by stranded travellers desparately trying to move on. Bus and truck companies were well aware of this and were becoming adept at exploiting the situation. When I left town Dave, demonstrating admirable leadership qualities, was still in the throws of trying to negotiate the hire of a bus to take the swelling ranks to the Chinese border post at Zhangmu. Everytime he thought he had a deal, the ground rules would change. Peter Fleming, in his account of the British Mission Force, reflects the British view of the Tibetans when he suggests, 'the Tibetan attitude was not in the least evasive or disingenuous; it was based four square on infantile obstinacy'. Obstinate they certainly could be as I was to discover every time I tried to negotiate transport or accommodation. It would appear that since the turn of the century they have also learnt a good deal of evasion and disingenuousness as well. When I think of it now, this seems a harsh judgement and reflects how locked into our western role expectations we can be.

The hotel manager was busy saving up for a trip to Dharmsala to see the Dalai Lama. With travel regulations more relaxed this was possible. This came as something of a surprise to me as I had expected the cross border traffic to be very much confined to outsiders. Some Tibetans were travelling to India, but what was more significant was that they were also coming back again. One of the ways the manager was saving was by having Panda tour groups shown round the hotel every afternoon. Since most of the residents were foreign budget travellers it was a 'bit of a con' showing this off as a typical Tibetan inn. It's a salutory role reversal situation to be on the receiving end, cornered by a group of camera clicking tourists.

The residents were an odd mix. The most memorable was a young Canadian sporting a long biblical beard, with hair in a ponytail, dressed in jungle outfit, all very neat and tidy as if he had just stepped out of a military outfitters. Everywhere he carried with him a bag of tsampa to feed himself on the road to adventure. He was in the process of teaming up with an American Buddhist nun, a timid Australian girl, a wacky German couple and a French follower of Bagwan Shree Rajneesh. They were planning to buy donkeys and carts to ride to Mt Kailas 1,000 the West. None of them had the first idea about one end of a donkey from another and had given no thought to what the donkeys, let alone themselves were going to eat–presumably tsampa. There was much pontificating about ways and means, giving the impression that all travellers who had come from Katmandu were terribly knowledgeable. So far they had bought one donkey, I'm sure to the delight of the seller, who had immediately struck a further deal to keep and feed the animal while their expedition plans progressed. Already the cracks in this bizarre alliance were miles wide. If not taken too seriously, their arguments and deliberations were light entertainment. Several of them had already been in Shigatze for over a month and the impression was that the summer would have slipped by before they made a move.

Much of Shigatze is a drab concrete Chinese city. The massive castle or dzong that dominated the old city was demolished stone by stone during the 1960's, presumably

78

because it was formerly a seat of regional authority. In contrast the Tashilumpo, the seat of the Panchen Lama, was left largely unharmed. Situated at 12,800 feet, it is the second largest city with a population of around 40,000. It lies at the confluence of the Brahmaputra *(Yarlong Tsangpo)* and the Liancuo *(Niang chu)* rivers. *Tashilhumpo* means 'heap of glory at the foot of Dromari' (Tara's mountain). It was founded in 1447 by Tsong Khapa's youngest disciple and nephew. At one time it had over 4,000 monks. Today there are 610 including 110 young novices. Many of these are very pushy. Tibetan travellers of former years frequently commented on what a brutal and licentious mob many of the monks were. These ones seemed primarily concerned with refilling their monastery's depleted coffers. Although I had Chinese identification papers, ten minutes argument made no dent in the gatekeeper's demand for 3 yuan entry. All Tibetans walk in and out freely. In a sense though this is perfectly fair. The wealth of the monasteries has been looted and, if they are to rebuild, or support more monks, then they need more money. Foreign tourists are one of the few obvious sources. They are ambivalent about whether they really want visitors at all. No doubt like stately homes fallen on hard times they feel they have no option, but this does not stop them from expressing their contempt at the same time as trying to milk the visitors for all they can get. In the Maitreya Temple *(Jamba Chyenmu)* I had my camera grabbed out of my hands even though I wasn't in the process of taking a photograph. It was then passed over the yak butter lamps, not at all good for the lens, and I was only able to get it back after handing over 20 yuan. However, I can hardly justify such peevishness, as I probably would have taken photographs without paying if I thought I could have got away with it. This temple was constructed in 1914 by the 9th Panchen Lama to house the Maitreya Buddha (the Buddha-to-come), a massive statue 83ft high and containing 614 lbs of gold.

In one of the halls a dong player blasted out the foghorn music I had heard at Ganden while novice monks *(trapas)* attempted to learn a ritual dance. Half were larking about and it did not impress as a very serious business. Maybe the atmosphere is lighter than in the days when the Lamas held the power of life and death. Maybe it was simply another expression of the Tibetans' innate ability to extract humour out of almost any situation.

Behind the Tashilhumpo a two mile pilgrim circuit winds round the hillside past prayer wheels and *mane* stones (sculpted or painted religious texts) from where there are fine views back down over the gold capped roofs. I later climbed the mountain behind and saw the whole valley floor on both sides; strung out between the rock faces on the summit a mass of prayer flags fluttered in the light breeze.

Our best bet for getting out of Shigatze looked like teaming up again with the pilgrims we had met first in Gyangtse. I had bumped into them in the Tashilumpo. They had been friendly and informed me they were staying across the road and that they would leave at 6 a.m. for Sakya monastery. They hoped to get there and back in a day, which we thought both improbable and optimistic. Anyway we slipped out of the hotel in the dead of night and made our way through the dog infested streets to the No. 1 Guesthouse. The gates of the Guesthouse were closed and there was no sign of life inside so we squatted down shivering, surrounded by packs of baying dogs. Nothing like a bit of local atmosphere at 5 a.m. After an hour, lights came on, engines started and the next thing we knew the gates opened and two trucks lumbered out into the street and we were left foolishly wondering what had happened. We'd blown it: another classic confusion between China time and Tibet time.

If there is a general shortage of dogs around in China, the opposite is true in Tibet. The first I had seen in Guangzhou were a pair, cooked whole, being wheeled through the market in a barrow. Many of my students in Kunming had eaten dog and assured me it was excellent, though I had refrained from testing this out in part from the sensitivities of a nation of dog lovers and part because I could not have looked my hound in the face on my return home. The streets of Lhasa are full of apparently contented beasts gnawing bones and watching life go by. The Tibetans believe dogs are often reincarnations of monks, which is one of the reasons why they are comparitively well treated. Around the monasteries the canine population seems to be completely out of control. Perhaps this is in direct relation to the thousands of monks who lost their lives during and after the uprising in 1959. It is a mystery what they all manage to live on. For the most part their condition is not too bad. There may be plenty of yak bones to gnaw in Lhasa, but this is hardly the case at the largely destroyed and deserted monasteries. The most likely explanation is that they are fed with scraps by the many pilgrims who are also generous with money for beggars.

As we had just witnessed not all the dogs were peaceful. At Naini monastery outside Gyangtse I had a chunk taken out of the knee of my jeans; fortunately the skin was not broken. No one seemed to be very clear about the risk of rabies but I had no wish to make a statistical contribution to this branch of medicine.

Conveniently, across from the hotel was the main covered market with an interesting selection of goods, both ancient and modern, everything from old coins, Yuan Shi-kai silver dollars to Tibetan currency of indeterminate age and value, goggles and bus drivers' gloves (wise purchases for what was to come), to amulets, rancid yak butter and prayer flags. Unfortunately the prices had already been corrupted by the regular arrival of Panda Tour Groups who seemed more than happy to hand over wads of FEC without any relation to the value of, or market rate for, the goods in question.

For homesick Han Chinese a street photographer had an impressive gallery of backdrops including a Red Flag limousine, a rare sight indeed in Tibet, as well as the Shanghai waterfront, perhaps a more realistic goal for most if they were ever to get back East again. The photographers commitment to private enterprise was no doubt commendable, but business appeared to be on the quiet side.

Shigatze offered a limited range of cuisine, though there was one reasonable Sichuan restaurant. I don't know whether it is because of population pressure, proximity, spirit of enterprise, or because they have been exiled, but the Sichuanese make up the bulk of the Chinese residents in Tibet and have established restaurants in most of the

81

population centres of any size. This suited me very well. The
other restaurant of note which I did not visit was innocently
mistranslated as the 'Restaurant of Good Smell'. A slight
problem here with the different meanings of *wei*, smell and
taste.

In an attempt to legitimise my intended journey west, I
made a visit with Dave to the Public Security Bureau which
has a special foreign affairs section. Here we were cordially
received. Dave made the early running.

"Hello – this is my comrade *Li Chade*. I'm *DaWei*. We're
both foreign teachers from Kunming. Can you help us?"

"What do you want?" "I'm on holiday and travelling to
Nepal which I wish to visit before returning to teach in
Kunming. But there's a problem. I need a re-entry visa for
China. I may not be able to get one in Katmandu and then I
would have to fly to Hong Kong and back to Kunming. This
would be very expensive."

"Yes, well, I'd like to help, but I don't have the necessary
stamp. Perhaps if you tried in Lhasa?"

"But I've just come from Lhasa."

"I see, I see." An embarrassed loss of face, as Dave made
some helpful remarks about what a pity this was, how much
he liked teaching and contributing to China's realising the
four modernisations, as I shot him a 'don't overdo it' glance.
This seemed like a good time to press forward my own claim.

"Maybe if you can't help my friend you could help me.
I'm returning to Britain via Pakistan and need to travel to
Kashi (Kashgar)."

"Why don't you fly?"

"Because I'd have to return to Lhasa, fly to Chengdu,
from Chengdu to Beijing, from Beijing to Wurumuqi
(Urumqi) and Wurumuqi to Kashi. This would be very
expensive and I'd be travelling at first in the wrong
direction."

"Yes, I see.– Well there are two roads to Kashi."

I thought he was going to refer to the Golmud-Urumqi route – but no –

"But they're both very bad, very dangerous. The southern route by Zhongba, Burang and Ali is blocked, and always very dangerous. You mustn't go that way."

"Well how about the northern road to Ali by Gerze and Gegyai?" Good thing I'd done my homework, I thought.

"Yes, well, if you avoid all risks and are very careful I can let you have a permit for the northern route." One of the ways to avoid taking risks he indicated was not to take any lifts with hard drinking Tibetan drivers. Although this was undoubtedly sound advice, if strictly followed it would make obtaining transport, extremely difficult at the best of times, nigh impossible. Although I knew quite a few foreigners had travelled through West Tibet, as far as I knew none besides tour groups had had permits, nonetheless possession of one gave me a sense of security and removed anxieties about being turned back, or of large fines at Yecheng. It was like having a 'Get Out Of Jail Free' card. Thus it was with inordinate pleasure that I left the office clutching a duly stamped permit for Kashgar, as far as I was aware the first one issued to an individual traveller. The permit didn't specify what route I was to take, so maybe this was a clever move on his part so that if trouble arose he could suggest he had expected me to travel by the usual route out of Tibet. It did, however, state the means of transportation *qiche* – literally steam vehicle – but encompassing all petrol and diesel vehicles, which in Tibet could mean only one thing – truck.

Dave seemed fairly certain that he could get the visa he needed either at the border post at Zhangmu, or in Katmandu itself, so he was able to contribute to my obtaining this important, if not vital piece of paper. One should never underestimate the value of official looking documents in China travel. Not only does it give you a much greater conviction in your arguments, but its authority, either real or imagined can often impress sufficiently to gain access, to smooth the path, to places others cannot reach. Depending on at whom the documents are targetted, they don't necesarily have to be genuine, although it is obviously better if they are. The degree to which counterfeit student cards have been used successfully throughout China bears witness to this.

The whole Chinese attitude to permits and travel is, to say the least, bizarre. In most countries with restricted areas, infringments lead to fines, imprisonment, or maybe worse. In China there have been allegations of spying, but they seem uncertain how to react to such an extent that there is no cohesive policy. This is in part because of the huge size of the country and also because of the very rapid pace of change. Up to 1984 most of China was still technically closed. It was only in late 1985 and early 1986 that travel permits ceased to have any particular relevance. A travelling companion told me he had approached the P.S.B. in Xiamen for travel permits and their most up to date list of open cities was gleaned from a back copy of the People's Daily.

Because of this uncertainty, acting illegally has been elevated to the status of a game by many travellers. A few have been fined, one or two even deported. More often than not they are simply put on the next bus or train out of town, but no one checks to see whether they then get off at the first halt and backtrack again. A few have achieved the distinctive honour of being required to write a self-criticism. This requires a bit of abject grovelling, along the lines of 'my grandfather would be deeply distressed and ashamed, as I am, to know that I have been acting so antisocially'. You lose face, the officials gain some, everyone is happy, maybe you can even continue on your way.

7

WERE ON A ROAD TO NOWHERE

After four days in Shigatze, I heard at ten at night from Bill and Denise, an American couple who has just arrived the day before, that they had an agreement, tentative as always, for a ride West at 5 a.m. the following morning. I was not really properly prepared, with limited food and wholly inadequate clothing, but this was certainly not a time for prevaricating. We arrived at the vehicle park at 5 a.m., but from previous experience did not expect any trucks to leave for an hour or so after the suggested time of departure. We were joined for a three hour vigil by Franz, a Dutchman, and Mileko, a Japanese girl. When there were eventually signs of life we identified the truck and found as well as being as heavily laden as it could conceivably be, that there were already three Tibetan passengers who had slept the night on the back of the truck. The day had to start predictably with an argument and attempts by one of the driver's two henchmen to throw Franz and Mileko off the truck. They were only travelling as far as Lhatse on the way to Nepal. The situation was finally resolved by them having to pay 10 yuan in advance. I had been advised that as a general principle it was a bad idea to part with any cash until at least half way to your destination.

At last, as the sun was coming up we were off. Perched precariously on the top of a lumpy cargo of potatoes, skins, plastic jerrycans, petrol drums and a host of other unidentifiable goods beneath us. Exposed to the elements, and cold at first, we warmed slowly as the bright sun began to burn across the arid semi-desert. Progress was slow. We averaged ten miles an hour for the next two days, but at least the slower you go the less bumpy it is. At this speed we enjoyed a superb vantage point from which to observe the passing countryside. In one sense there was very little to see. In another plenty: the subtly changing skies, the dramatic scale of the wilderness, the incredibly hardy nomadic herdsmen who appeared in the middle of nothing walking purposefully towards nothing, above all the quality of the light, reminiscent of a surrealist painting. Except there is a brightness, a clarity to it that cannot be caught on canvas, perhaps not even on film. This I nonetheless endeavoured to do, but felt, as I have often before, that I was maybe trespassing, trying to trap the soul of the place, to reduce it to manageable and comprehensible proportions.

We crossed over another pass, this one at 14,000 feet and learnt the Tibetan cry of 'La so lo', a cry of ecstasy on achieving the summit. The Tibetans have a natural sense of fun. They like to laugh, and amongst themselves do so a lot. They are not keen, however to accept strangers and at first can be downright unfriendly. The response when doing the rounds looking for a lift can lead quite quickly to a state of nervous depression, which seemed to have paralysed travellers in both Lhasa and Shigatze into a state of total inaction. One thing abundantly clear from the outset was that the prime motive for giving you a lift was to get as much money from you as they could. Even if you have paid and Tibetan passengers have not, you are at the bottom of the pecking order. That's the way it is.

At Lhatze we were dropped off before the village as there was reputed to be a P.S.B. checkpoint. We walked into the centre and stopped at a cafe for a meal of rice and potatoes. Foreigners only get fed after all the Tibetans have been served (the same usually applies to Han Chinese as well) so you are constantly having to rush your food down before being hustled back to the truck, not good for the nerves or the digestion. The cafe was full with a busload of foreigners on the way up from Zhangmu. Covered in dust they looked as much of a mess as we did although they were travelling inside a bus; but then not all the buses have a full complement of windows. Our driver joined us in the cafe and we then walked out to the other side of the village to rejoin the truck. I can't believe that any P.S.B. present would have been fooled by this manoeuvre.

Franz and Mileko dropped off here, which gave us a little more space. A couple of miles on we came to the Tsangpo, which was crossed on a large winch drawn ferry. We only had to wait an hour or so, which was good going. Long delays we had heard were more the rule than the exception.

Setting off on the far side I had a feeling of great excitement, tinged with an appreciable degree of anxiety. We were entering a large area of still barely charted wilderness. Despite my permit this was really forbidden territory. Traditionally inhabited by Drogpas (Nomads) who are preyed on by robber bands, the niceties of Western civilisation, the value of paper credentials, suddenly became supremely irrelevant. We were very much at the mercy of our driver. He had so far not proved to be too unfriendly and I had been able to converse with him a little in Chinese, but one of his henchmen impressed as particularly unsavoury. Gap toothed and sporting a felt hat, he had glowered at us at every possible opportunity. These felt hats are very popular with the Tibetans. They are close to those worn by Australian Diggers, but with the Tibetan mongoloid features, dark skin and weather burnt complexion, they look very like Red Indians. All that childhood conditioning of westerns on television gave me a lurking suspicion that I was about to be scalped at any moment. I thought I'd better keep my wits about me. He had been the one most forceful in trying to eject Franz and Mileko before we first set off.

The three Tibetans who travelled on the back of the truck with us spoke little and only in Tibetan. They wore western style brown suitings with thin polo-neck jerseys and disguised their expressions behind dark sun glasses. Encouraged by how we were initially treated, however, they occcupied the prime positions and made no move to share out the available space equitably. This I discovered was the norm. You push, poke, wriggle and shove your way into the best possible position. They are not above simply sitting down on top of you. Survival of the fittest is the order of the day. As you cross successive pain thresholds on your cramped perch you adapt quickly to the need to fight for your own corner.

Black thoughts about your immediate neighbour can easily develop. With little else to occupy your mind, it is easy to become paranoid. Conversation is not always easy as you bump and grind along. The magnitude of the surroundings also tends to encourage a degree of introspection. Travelling on a Liberation truck *(Jiefang)* in West Tibet is perhaps a little like being the crew of a moon buggy. It's all a bit daunting. The scenery is desolate, moonscape imagery; stone, dust, brown, unforgiving. Like moonwalking, the first step was a giant step into a new world, into the unknown. I could no longer even pretend to myself that I was sure of what I was doing and why I was doing it. The aloofness of the Tibetans gave me no encouragement. Bill and Denise were still very much an unknown quantity. So far all I had managed to glean was that he had money in property in California which only required collecting from time to time and so they had the leisure to be professional travellers.

Jiefang are the backbone of the Chinese trucking fleet. The original design was American. They gave it to the Russians during the Second World War, who in turn gave it to the Chinese. It appears to have a limited number of moving parts, and so although breakdowns are frequent it doesn't require a high technology genius to fix them. The most useful tool for repairs is possibly the crowbar. Most of the Jiefangs in Tibet were on their last legs, which was one of the reasons for their very slow progress. Remarkably though, they eventually reach their destination and have proved to be impressive beasts of burden.

On the whole the Tibetans are not the best of drivers, although I would certainly not accuse them of being timid. The hills on the passes are not particularly steep, having been built with long zig-zagging gradients, no doubt with the Jiefang's limitations in mind, When going up hill the mechanic and his mate, the surly Red Indian lookalike, frequently leapt off and ran behind the truck, putting stones behind the wheels. On sharp bends progress was made by a series of blocked fits and starts. It was not helped by the driver insisting on waiting until he had practically stalled before changing gear, and then often proceeding to do so. I may, however, be judging him unfairly, as any vestiges of syncromesh, if there ever were such a thing, must have long since disappeared. The rock crew thought this the greatest of fun and improved their humour to the extent that they began to grin at us, and we grinned back. We were not going to be scalped after all. Whereas we spend much of our time being deadly serious, the Tibetans spend much of theirs laughing. It is central to their nature. We thought such erratic progress was a problem to be overcome. They found it a source of great amusement. I had much to learn from such a different set of values.

At Sangsang we dropped off the three Tibetan passengers and were glad to have sufficient space to stretch out and also to huddle down with a little shelter. At about 6 p.m. we stopped to change a wheel. None of the tyres had any visible tread on them when we set out and one had now shredded. This lack of tread did not help on the passes which were damp enough to send the wheels spinning.

Changing the wheel only took four hours and involved an instructive if primitive approach to the problem. A jammed nut was attacked with brute force, a blow torch (burnt half the tyre), hammer and crowbar. The final successful solution was half an hour with a file. I helped in this process which greatly improved our standing. For the last hour thunder had been booming and a storm was obviously rapidly approaching. Blue sky turned to an ominous grey. There were no trees, no shrubs, not even a blade of grass in which to read the wind speed. I felt very vulnerable lacking even these tell-tale pointers to the weather. The driver himself suggested we might try to hitch a ride if anything came past. A truck did eventually appear with an empty cab, but the driver demanded 30 yuan each to take us the last hour or two to the next truckstop. We were paying 25 yuan for two days (or however long it took) to Raka, so we declined this extortionate offer.

On our way again at about 10 p.m. we finally arrived at Kaka at midnight. For the last hour we had sheltered as best we could from the sleet and hail under a plastic sheet and a blanket . It was with considerable relief that we finally stumbled into a truckstop room. The heavens opened as we closed the door behind us and lit the candle. We were frozen through and it was becoming clear to me that I was totally unprepared for these kind of conditions with no sleeping bag and only a thin anorak; another mountain leadership failure. Bill and Denise's blanket had made all the difference. It bought to mind the Highlander's use of the plaid which even when soaked through provided some protection from the elements. The greatest life saver, which was to prove its worth over the next months was a pair of Chinese silk long-johns. I had never envisaged myself being the proud owner of such a garment, but I can think of silk now as being worth its weight in gold. The warmest possible material next to your skin, it is also pleasantly cool when the day heats up. Travelling in Tibet in summer with a very wide range of temperature, it is the ideal material.

The next day we left Kaka at 10 a.m., a leisurely start to the day. Most of it was spent trying to shelter from the rain under the inadequate plastic sheet, as we again got progressively colder. Besides wondering whether I was going to freeze to death I started to worry about the long term success of Chinese dentistry as I was now definitely 'beyond the pale'. In Kaifeng I had had a second tooth filled; the first having been repaired a couple of weeks previously at Yunnan University. This had reassured me that although the hygiene was hardly up to Western standards the dentists seemed reasonably competent and the machinery, drills etc. little different from those used by my dentist at home, dating probably from the 1960's.

Through Liz's university interpreter Zhou Li, I had an address and a name. The lady in question was not in at the first establishment and at the second I was examined by someone else. This was a serious linguistic test, as any misunderstanding could, I felt, have dire consequences for me. This is where pocket dictionaries are next to useless, but no other interpretation was available.

The examining dentist appeared to be saying it was serious and that he would have to give me some medicine and then wait for a week before he could do any work. Besides the fact that I had not anticipated being in town so long, this did not sound at all encouraging. What kind of medicine do you take that acts for a whole week? Was this going to be some sort of general anaesthetic and was he going to remove half my teeth? My apprehension was also increased by the fact that the dental chairs were in two rows of six in one large room, suggesting mass dentistry by numbers. This reduces dentistry to the level of a visit to the barber. The old barber's red and white pole signifying blood-letting might have been more appropriate. Discretion being the better part of valour, I suggested that at this stage that perhaps I should withdraw and return the next day with Zhou Li as interpreter. So the next day we started at the first dental centre looking for a Mrs Zhou. A Mrs Zhou duly came forward but subsequently turned out not to be the one who had been so highly recommended by the other foreign teachers.

Although in mid-operation on another patient she immediately turned her attention to my tooth, drilled out the broken filling and with only a few twinges of pain the huge hole was filled. I was almost more concerned about the surroundings than the actual operation itself. In one corner was the hapless lady left in mid operation, but in fact she seemed quite content to observe a foreigner under the drill. Not so easy to keep a stiff upper lip here. At the other end another girl was having an injection of what looked like all of four inches of some dark blue liquid. The lamp stand, which was broken, crashed to the ground at the first attempted adjustment. The lamp was thereafter held by a young assistant, which might be one way to deal with overmanning in the dental services.

Liz helpfully pointed out the encrusted blood splattered down the side of the chair and, for spitting out those crunched up, drilled-out bits of filling, there was one of those spittoon basins seen all over China, half-full of all kinds of dubious looking swabs, etc. which did not bear closer examination. However, for prompt service, a competent filling and a great relief from anxiety travelling through China 6.50 yuan (just over £1.) seemed a small price to pay.

Investigating dentistry had become a bit of an obsession for me. At the street level hideous looking operations are performed. A public spectacle not for the squeamish. I recall having been horrified by the treadle drill one of my uncles, a dentist in England, used to use for home visits in the days before urban electricity became universal. These infernal machines are standard equipment as are a scarifying range of pliers, pincers and other tools of the trade. To advertise their services there are often grinning rows of false teeth in jam jars. Some display a ghoulish collection of their successful extractions. In comparison with all this my ordeal seemed most tame.

In the late afternoon we were dropped off at Raka. Payment made without rancour, incongruous handshakes with the driver and they were off on the south road to Zhongba. To heighten the feeling of abandonment we had to deal with an officious, rude and unhelpful *fuwu yuan*. We were the only people so far staying the night. He immediately took my *gongzuo zheng* (work card) and refused to return it until we left. Although this is not uncommon practice, the manner in which it was done did not bode well and gave the impression that we were being imprisoned. We were charged 4 yuan a head for a mud floored room with an inoperable stove and no fuel. To cap it all he refused to give us any *kai shui* (boiled water), so all that we had had that day were '761' biscuits. These are, I think, porkfat based Chinese army rations; a form of hardtack. The taste takes a little getting used to, but they fight off the hunger pangs and proved a good source of energy. I had bought four packets in Shigatze, and was to regret later that I had not bought a whole lot more.

Later that night some Sichuanese truck drivers pulled in and gave us some fish they had caught on the way down. Most Tibetans neither fish for, nor eat, fish. The Sichuanese have no such Buddhist scruples. The fish was pressure cooked with chillies to make a fiery soup, bones and all, but was much appreciated.

Two more trucks pulled in later on their way to Gerze but refused to take us although they had plenty of room. They weren't even prepared to give us the time of day and we darkly suspected that the fuwu yuan was not unconnected with such overt hostility. At 14,400 feet it was very cold at night and my breathing was laboured. In the morning we were reluctant to leave our beds. Outside fresh snow covered the hills. There was no transport and no indication that the *fuwu yuan* was going to become any more helpful.

Zemne ban (what's to be done)? A bit of pluck required, what? Bill with appropriate inspiration produced a frisbee and we started to warm up, breathlessly panting after the frisbee which performed most impressively in the thin atmosphre. From accounts of the British Mission Force footballs behave likewise and it bought to mind Alexandra David-Neal's tales of 'leaping Lamas'. She was the first Western woman to reach Lhasa in October 1923 disguised as a pilgrim. She was much ridiculed for her fantastic tales of Lamas flying across the plains in a series of spectacular leaps and, because of this, sceptics doubted many of her other claims. Perhaps these criticisms were unduly unkind after all.

Not much point in standing in the road. Nowhere to walk to. The junction could have been miles further on. The plateau stretched away for miles on either side to low lines of hills. Around the truckstop mud walls lay the usual depressing collection of refuse, excreta and bits of yak and sheep. If they are keen to develop tourism, Raka has a few improvements to make.

Baden-Powell advocated in 'Scouting For Boys' the great importance of 'a good rear' at least twice daily for a healthy mind and body. We forget as modern day backpackers what a serious matter this was for our forbears, not least for former Asia travellers who frequently had porters to carry mountains of luggage including wicker commodes.

The more widely you travel in China the worse the toilets you will meet. One accepts that privacy is an unnatural state for the Chinese, but in this country a new meaning is given to the 'public' in public convenience. For most Westerners the lack of both privacy and basic hygiene is an initial shock that some would-be travellers never overcome. However distasteful you may find it though, by the time you leave China you will undoubtedly have come to terms with your own faeces. If this is basically true of China, by the time you have left Tibet you will also have had to face up to a lot of other people's as well.

Hygiene appears to be an unknown concept in Tibet. About the first observation in some of the earliest accounts of Tibet has been what a dirty race the Tibetans are. These comments were written at a time when most of the rest of the world was hardly noted for its high standards. Whereas there have been improvements elsewhere in this matter, some might argue in the West, to an unnatural, prudish and obsessive degree, Tibet appears to have made no progress at all. Tibetans wear their grime like a second skin, further protection against the elements. With no opportunity to wash and incessant coatings of dust I was coming closer to an understanding of their condition.

Fortunately for the Tibetans the altitude and exceptional aridity, coupled with a short warm summer means that flies do not thrive. If it were not for this fact they would most certainly have been wiped out by plagues many times over. Unfortunately both lice and bedbugs appear immune to these rigours of climate and find a most agreeable habitat for themselves.

Among travellers the effect of having to live with these extremely primitive conditions and the prevalence, if not universality, of internal disorders, is that bodily functions are discussed in much the same way as the British discuss the weather. It is a topic of major interest. Everyone has a view, everyone is involved.

Just as we were beginning to tire of frisbee, a green mail van trundled up from the Zhongba direction, stopped and disgorged three foreigners and what seemed like a mountain of luggage. Not quite Dr Livingstone, but definite shades of same. The first out was a tall blond Dutchman, Zop van Dyke, an art dealer from Amsterdam, followed by Peta Cross, a nurse from Hobart, Tasmania, and last Don Rose, a contractor from California.

Zop and Peta had been stuck at Parayang 125 miles west

for two weeks trying to get through to Mt Kailas. When all other avenues had failed, they bought two yaks, but after several days of trying every method from prayer to violence still found them quite unmanageable. They had had to sell them again at a loss.

Don had been making his way west by horse and a home-made cart that he had ingeniously cobbled together in Shigatze. After a month of solitary travelling he had been defeated by high rivers. Zop and Peta were the first foreigners he had seen for three weeks, and now in the same day three more.

Under the more experienced guidance of these seasoned West Tibetan wanderers we dined well on *tukba* a composite stew of noodles, tsampa and whatever other ingredients were proffered. When the opportunity arose this was how we ate for the next few days. Tongues were loosened. The *fuwu yuan* turned out to have a supply of beer, matches and sweets, though nothing else. We were soon discovering each others life histories.

It is of course a very small world, but for coincidences a meeting in Raka takes some beating. It turned out Peta and I had a close mutual aquaintance from Hobart. For some strange reason a few years previously several people from the same 'scene' there made their way independently to the North of Scotland, a reverse deportation. They all ended up living on the Black Isle in Ross-Shire. It was with these people that Peta had grown up. What is more she had recently been working in a hospital in Launceston where one of my Scots cousins had been for the last year. This was obviously a meeting of some significance. I was to travel with Zop and Peta for the next month.

Under normal circumstances one's domestic arrangements are often a matter of meticulous consideration and intricate planning. Choosing to live with another person or persons is not something to be taken lightly. Part of the fun of travelling is that by accident rather than design family can develop almost instantaneously. Relationships are direct, perhaps uncompromising, but also uncluttered with the complications of a more static existence. The time scale is kaleidoscoped.

95

8

DON'T MENTION THE WAR

Late that evening a German Tour Group appeared with four Toyota landcruisers and a brand new Izuzu fuel injection truck, over which we positively drooled. This must be the way to travel. All the approaches to the other half dozen trucks that had passed or stopped had been unsuccessful. There was much speculation as to whether they would take us and what the best approach would be. Zop as a speaker of German was despatched to fraternise whilst we almost indecently hovered around trying to find out how he was getting on.

It was an absurd drawn out game. It was perfectly obvious we were stuck and that they were the ones to help us. They, however, had paid £4–5,000 a head for a three week round trip from Katmandu to Mt Kailas. We must have seemed a most unwelcome and wild looking bunch of freeloading 'hippy' types. It was not surprising that they were not over keen to take us. We therefore set out to impress them that appearances were deceptive and that we were really very nice people. This was a bit difficult when they didn't want to speak to us and we didn't speak their language.

It was not until the morning that the issue was settled. Their tour leader agreed to take us as long as the Chinese liaison officer did not object. Having cleared that hurdle we then left to negotiate with the Tibetan truck driver who was eventually beaten down to 70 yuan each. 420 yuan for doing nothing was not bad for him. We both knew a deal was on, but as Heinrich Harrer noted, 'during the months of our sojourn in Tibet, we had become better acquainted with the mentality of Asiatics and knew that to give way early was against the rules'.

So off again on another twelve hour ride. The junction of

96

17. Drogpa boy with discarded rum bottle. Tunghu.

18. Drogpa at Mt Kailas.

19. Old Drogpa at salt lake. Tunghu.

20. Khampa pilgrims on truck to Kailas.

21. The valley of Amitabha. Kailas.

22. Pilgrim mother and children at Kailas river crossing.

23. Drogpa women at Kailas.

24. Kailas. North face.

the only two roads in the whole of West-Central Tibet was not even marked, except that from the time we turned north, rough track·would be an over-generous description of the route. Whenever it was in the least feasible our driver drove like a maniac, racing against the land cruisers. Travelling on this new truck wasn't so wonderful after all.

It was hot, dry and dusty. Our lips cracked. Half the time we could hardly see. But then you couldn't really see out over the back anyway. Three of the 50 gallon fuel drums leaked and two came adrift and rolled around the back. We all climbed up on top of the camper mats as far to the front as we could go, to avoid either being crushed or asphyxiated. This in turn led to complaints that we were crushing the Germans' vegetables, which created further ill feeling.

In compensation the tour group, which was composed mainly of naturalists and botanists, stopped at every available site of interest which we would have otherwise missed. These included some hot springs south of Coquen where several Drogpa yurts were pitched. It was strangely like something out of a science fantasy film with primitive nomads milking yaks next to hot spring geysers. It all reinforced the moonscape imagery. The traditional division in work roles appeared to be followed here. The women were busy with the yaks. The men stood around looking decorative. This they do extremely well, having a natural studied indifference.

Further on whilst we were being pulled out by another truck from getting stuck in the middle of a river, a kiang (wild ass) was spotted galloping a long way off across the hillside. These fine animals used to be a familiar sight. Officers in the British Mission Force wrote of herds ten to twenty strong turning and wheeling with military precision out on the plain. Now they are a threatened species. It is claimed the P.L.A. gunned most of them down for sport and for meat. There is little enough in this wilderness. It is all the poorer for the near elimination of much of its wild life. There were still some rare sights to be seen like the four blue wild sheep (burrhel) moving with grace and agility that the group's sirdar spotted high up on a rock face.

Uli, the tour leader, was a fund of useful information on

these subjects. He identified the birds we had seen on the road to Raka as black necked cranes. Had I even a nodding aquaintance with botany I could have gleaned a great deal about the few plants that grow in the region. This was the most clement time of year and a number of unusual flowers were emerging: I had noticed purple leafless blossoms that hugged the ground. Even now the grass was spiky and very sparse, so that the Drogpa were constantly on the move with their flocks in search of better grazing. What do they do in the winter? I don't know. There is no visible system of gathering winter fodder. How anyway could it be stored by nomads with no housing or permanent shelters? Presumably livestock get very thin. There must be more hospitable parts than this desolation. There are certainly no melons on the Chang Tang. It is a vast desert wilderness, roughly 1,500 miles long and 400 miles wide, more than 500,000 square miles in all. From almost anywhere it is a very long way to fairer pastures and, on the plateau itself, there is no question of being able to descend to find grazing.

At the end of the first day with the tour group we arrived at Coquen, another mudfloored truckstop by a river with a few houses packed closely together. Here Bill and Denise met Carl, a young blonde Dutch punk, with whom they had travelled in East Tibet. They themselves had come to Lhasa from Chengdu, but Carl had made rapid progress on the even more difficult route from Lijiang in West Yunnan. He had a lift in a jeep for the morning and preferred to travel on independently. I mention his blondness because this more than anything else makes foreigners stand out as belonging to some totally different species. Both Zop and Peta were similarly blonde which later tended to undermine my attempts to blend in subtly.

We didn't get away from Coquen until 11.30 a.m. Many of the tour group were far from happy with the accommodation and even in the relative comfort of landcruisers were exhausted from the previous long day of being bounced up and down. There were more arguments about packing, petrol fumes, dust and broken ropes and the ill feeling this generated was exacerbated by one of the German women suggesting that we were their guests, implying we ought to be more grateful for the lift. Being patronised by rich Germans was hardly what I came to Tibet for. (I've yet to decide what I was really there for adventure, self-discovery, its romantic mystery, its inaccessability, because it is there, because it was ordained?)

So who am I? Why am I here? I have assumed, taken it for granted even, that everyone would want to visit far flung places, in physical space even more than in a spiritual sense. I find myself drawn to that which is different, maybe a little odd, and relish an innate eccentricity. It has been argued true eccentrics are among the happiest citizens and are not we all seeking happiness?

'Walk on' were Gautama Buddha's last words to his disciples. Wandering is in our genes. The Tibetan definition for a human heing is *a-gro ba*, one who goes on migrations. At first we were nomads. Bruce Chatwin, chronicling nomadism in 'The Songlines', observes that babies start to cry as soon as their carrier stops. We are arguably at our best, at our happiest when we are walking. But it is also hard work. He notes that travel is also 'travail, bodily or mental labour, toil, especially of a painful or oppressive nature, hardship, suffering. A journey? From the Buddhist perspective, life is a journey rife with suffering, the Samsaric existence.

By 1986 travel to China seemed almost commonplace and so my journey was not simply to impress or to gain acclaim; but I cannot deny a search for a personal sense of achievement, to do something truly memorable, perhaps unique, to visit places few others have reached in what seems like a rapidly shrinking world. Initially this ambition had not expanded so far as to encompass Tibet. At times I have felt I should have been born in an earlier age, with wider physical horizons. My brief military career might have made more sense to me in such a context, whereas I joined in 1968, a year in which despite many important developments on the international scene, British military activity was distinctly limited. BAOR and Aldershot were only odd in relation to my peers who were busily exploring 'sex, drugs and rock and roll'.

The military training and conditioning, albeit rejected as a career, gave me an impetus and motivation for climbing mountains and travelling. If I start I intend to finish. However uncomfortable, I will look for others first to provide the excuse for not continuing – often a relief when they do, and the stiff upper lip can thankfully be abandoned. Getting from A to B involves practical issues and is, I find, an absorbing process – the difficulties and discomforts a challenge to be met and overcome. All this, consciously and subconsciously, becomes a voyage of personal discovery, a coming to terms with self in relation to the world: seeing is believing.

Feelings were running high with another day of acute discomfort ahead of us. With the repacking of the truck we had been forced down to the back with progressively less and less in the way of cushioning. After a few hours you develop a method of suspended animation. You begin to be able to read the engine revs and the feel of the truck and, with almost second sight, can anticipate the next spine-juddering crunch. We all got very good at clutching onto supports or each other even when half asleep. Considering the cramped, uncomfortable and even dangerous conditions, it is a great credit to the whole party that mutterings about each others' assumed more comfortable positions were kept to a minimum. At one stage of the journey, when we gave a huge Khampa a lift for a few hours, he, if anything, looked even more miserable than we did, so it wasn't simply a matter of soft Westerners.

The second night we stopped at Tunghu, a large lake with glistening white borax deposits lining the shores of its turquoise water. I claim this as Tunghu, but in all honesty map-reading is guesswork on the Chang Tang. Zop had a set of American aviation maps which were far the most detailed available. They were quite good for relief, but names and a few tracks marked seemed most arbitrary. The second of Eric Shipton's Six Mountain Travel Books, 'Blank on the

Map', describes his exploration of the northern Karakoram. 'In this shrinking world, where original exploration is perhaps now only possible on a journey into the inner mind,' he suggests, 'Central Tibet offers one of the few remaining such blank spaces. A rare treat not to know where you are, even after a careful perusal of the available maps.'

No one in the party had been this way before. The Chinese liaison officer was way out of his depth and a couple of thousand miles from home. At some stage during the day we must have met the track in from the East, but this was in no way apparent on the ground. On most maps this approach to West Tibet is not even marked at all. It is only after 1959 that any real transport infrastructure has existed and the Chinese have been in no hurry to publish detailed maps of exactly what does exist. Many of the routes in any case only open for part of the year, although paradoxically it is in the summer that roads are most likely to be cut when the rains get through. In winter the intense cold may freeze the drivers if not the trucks, but because of the exceptional aridity there is little snow. On the routes like this one there are no bridges. If the rivers swell the way is impassable and a new crossing place must either be discovered or you have to wait until the river goes down. There is little transport on the move. At the time this was the only open route (just) to the West, but most days we saw less than a dozen vehicles going either way.

Most vehicles sensibly travel in convoys. The exception was a bus that was taking a whole party of Sichuanese Geothermal engineers from Lhasa to Ali, where they were destined to spend the next couple of years. I had talked to a few when they stopped the night at Raka and none of them seemed particularly keen on the prospect of a long period of exile in the wilderness. After a few days on the road they were even less enthusiastic. The old Chinese buses are basically Jiefang engines and chassis with a metal box and seats welded on top. When we caught up with them first at a river crossing, it seemed a miracle they had managed to get so far, let alone to have crossed the river in which we in our brand new Izuzu proceeded to get stuck.

At Tunghu, Zop and Peta pitched their tent while the rest

of us prepared to sleep out. The feeling of separation and opposition was physically reinforced by our encampment a hundred yards from the tour group whose tents had been erected by the Sherpas. They sat down to roast lamb purchased from, and slaughtered by, the Drogpas, whose large flock was grazing by the lakeside. Although by religion the Tibetans are primarily vegetarians, life on the Chang Tang without eating meat would be untenable. Consequently they are very much more conscious of the fact that the animal is being sacrificed for their own existence. A slaughter is accompanied by prayers and incantations. Nothing is left, nothing is wasted.

The Germans sat on tubular steel chairs and washed their lamb down with bottles of rum. We squatted on the ground impatiently waiting for another *tukba* to cook. The general feeling was that if the level of animosity was to remain the same, then we did not wish to continue with the tour group. Perhaps it was largely our own foolish pride. Realistically we could hardly demand to be left where we were, even if we could have got some of our money back.

As the sun was going down Uli. came across and did a masterly job of reassuring us and diffusing some of our pent up fury. He explained that he had travelled much himself, having been first to Nepal in 1968, staying for a year and a half. He had since been back many times, spoke some Tibetan and had come to follow Buddhism. Both from his own experience and because he had two sons who had hitched about, he fully appreciated the difficulties that could so easily arise between two such different groups. He predicted that in a few days time they would warm to us, as he obviously had, and that we would have much we could share in terms of experience and knowledge. He was happily to prove correct in his assessment.

As I have already noted, with no sleeping bag I was not exactly well prepared for sleeping out at 15,000 feet. Even with Zop's Tibetan wool coat (*tschuba*) I spent a very cold night, but in compensation the panorama of stars was quite the most fantastic I have ever seen. I suppose it helped being a few thousand feet closer to them. The first half of the night was passed in metaphysical speculation on infinity, a quest I thought I had given up a long time ago as a waste of time. But what more fitting surroundings with distant electrical storms flashing to the south over the Himalayas. The dawn was slow but indescribably beautiful. There is an unparallelled quality to this, the most remote corner of 'the roof of the world'.

Before we left everyone conscientously cleared up. The Drogpa were back and made off with anything they thought they could use. Since there is nothing in this countryside, almost anything is judged worthy of taking back to their yurts. I photographed a young boy carrying off an empty bottle of rum. This on one level was a worrying foretaste of the impact of Western tour group so-called civilisation on the local culture, but on another it simply provided a welcome container for a people who have the meanest of bare necessities.

We stopped later on for a picnic lunch by a river near Oma, where there were a series of strange stupa shaped mud buildings, presumably store houses for a couple of fields of stunted barley growing by the trackside. By nightfall we reached Yan hu Chu (Salt Lake Place), passing close by Thok Yalung the fabled goldfields where the Tibetans mined the gold for their temples. One of their greatest fears was that if they allowed foreigners in, they would destoy their religion and steal their gold. The foreigners who subsequently marched in and did precisely that were the Chinese. There is no information available as to what is happening now at the gold fields.

For a pleasant change the truckstop rooms were reasonably clean and the management friendly. Zop had bought a leg of lamb in Gerze and this, cooked up with dried mushrooms, noodles and a tin of sardines made an original and reviving feast. Very tired from the dustiest, bumpiest and most exhausting truck ride so far, I slept like a log.

What was supposed to be the first picnic stop on the next day's run turned out to be rather more. Our truck driver drove into the middle of a field by a small settlement and prompty got bogged. In true local driving style he revved his engine and spun the wheels back and forth until the back axle disappeared into the ground. Apparently satisfied with his work, he then got out and devoted his attention to a brew up. The Germans were far from amused, started looking at their watches and disclaiming loudly about time schedules – time schedules in West Tibet?

This was the moment to tip the scales in our own favour. Don, Zop, Bill and I took turns with the spades digging out the back wheels and dropping in rocks. Two landcrusiers were hitched on and eventually out the Izuzu came.

'Das ist wunderbar'. The superiority of Western skill and application had been amply demonstrated, the problem resolved. The delay now a minor irritation. How to achieve an instant metamorphosis from despised travelling bum to fine upstanding adventurers in the historically heroic mould. Our stock with the Germans had risen considerably. Fraternisation between the parties began, addresses exchanged, a little of their surplus lunch even came our way. During the course of this merry intercourse Uli informed me that he had Scots ancestry. His grandmother was none other than a Bain from Dingwall, my home town. She had gone out to Argentina where she had married a German. Great concern was now expressed about the poor packing of the truck and the leaking fuel drums. The truck driver was firmly told to get his house in order.

One of the problems of the aridity is continually cracking lips. Denise had a dreadful time with her contact lenses. At first we all wrapped scarves around our mouths and those that had them wore an interesting variety of goggles. Later we were included in the .tour group handout of surgical masks, making us look like a particularly desparate theatre team. None of these, however, provided much protection against the all pervasive dust.

Although our exact position was uncertain, it now looked as if we would make Ali by nightfall, and indeed we at last started to descend towards the Indus river. On the river banks there were even a few scrubby bushes. After the last week these stood out like beacons on the path to an oasis. It dawned on me why the Islamic paradise has both water and shade. This brings to mind the delightful story of a group of Moors taken on a countryside trip to a waterfall in France. The guide told them it was time to go, but they were remarkably loathe to move, eventually explaining that they were waiting for the end, so miraculous was the spectacle to these desert dwellers.

Ali is hardly an oasis in this mould. Situated on the banks of the Indus, it is the Han administrative capital of West Tibet. Technically the region is now Ali and the town Shiquanhe (Lion spring river), but you will be lucky to find either name on most maps. Traditionally Gartok, 30 miles south was the most important trade and administrative centre and capital of the former province of Ngari. Ali has been built from scratch in the last twenty years, initially as a garrison town straddling the North-South, East-West road links. A population figure of about 3,000 was mentioned. Much of the town is of standard Han concrete construction. It even boasts a bank, a post office, a three storey supermarket and a new hotel built to accommodate passing tour groups, geothermal engineers and any party of functionaries having the misfortune to be sent on business to this, one of the most far flung outposts of the Chinese Empire.

Given its remote situation and the great difficulties experienced in getting there, Ali has a lot going for it. For us this was fortunate as we were to spend rather more time there than we had either anticipated or desired.

There are plenty of exotica in the Ali market place and the foreigners must have rated as an interesting addition. There is really no middle ground. Either there are expensive tour groups or budget travellers. This immediately creates conflicts. The hotel standards are hardly up to tour group expectations and budget travellers are not used to being asked for 50 yuan for a bed. The racial mix is unusual with Xinjiang Uyghurs, Han Chinese and Tibetans. Maybe because the Han, although conquerors, are neither in the .majority, nor secure in their domination, there is a feeling of much easier intercourse between the different parties than in,for instance,Lhasa. The majority of the P.L.A. garrison appear to be from Xinjiang or Gansu, Han frontiersmen pushing west like the Americans in the 19th century. This intermix makes for a lively market, Khampa tents cheek by jowl with the Muslim bread kiln. On the other side were the

105

Sichuan restaurants for a whole range of excellent cuisine. I tried *fanqie jidan* (tomato - scrambled eggs) with Muslim bread for breakfast. There are also coffee and tea shops and a couple of places for games of *Xiangqi* where Zop and I whiled away many pleasant hours.

A Chinese friend in Kunming had initially taught me Xiangqi, usually translated as Chinese Chess. Although *Xiang* is the character for elephant it is in fact one of the least important pieces on the board, or maybe there is a subtlety here that has totally eluded me. I had purchased a magnetic travelling set which helped break the ice on several long journeys. Like Ma Jong the Chinese tend to play it both fast and aggressively. A major problem is that they are pathologically incapable of allowing you to play your own game. One accepts that foreigners pretending they have mastered such a complicated Chinese game is naturally a spectacle of great interest, but we did not feel we had to have a group of P.L.A. men make every move for us. No lack of advice was available.

Excited cries of *'chi ma, chi ma'*, literally 'eat horse' (take his knight) would interrupt our concentration. At times we had to restrain the onlookers from arguing with each other over the next move and who was going to make it, not one of us, one of them. Having observed several of their own games it became apparent that this was not necessarily patronising the stupid foreigners. They muscle in on each other's games all the time too. My only regret was that in my entire time in China I never succeeded in beating a single Chinaman. At one restaurant there was the authentic atmosphere of yak butchered at the table. For the terminally home-sick one could buy Chinese half-filled tubes of smarties.

On arrival we left the tour group at the Ali hotel and managed to get a couple of rooms in the guesthouse. We dined next door on *jiaozi* and *tudou* (potatoes). There were already half a dozen foreigners in residence including Japanese and Americans. The next day a truck with thirteen more arrived from Lhasa. So much for a closed area. You are not supposed to be in West Tibet at all and yet it is rated one of the best places for visa extensions. You are of course in a strong position to argue that you will need at least another month to get out of China. For Ali this might even be an underestimate. Some people had obtained permits for Mt Kailas, but a 50 yuan kickback was being demanded for these, so no one was trying to get them any more. For the first two or three days we didn't even consider making plans to move on. Necessary recovery time is about equal to time spent on the road. Cleanliness is hardly uppermost in your mind on this kind of journey. Fortunately the dry atmosphere inhibits sweat and although I never saw a Tibetan ever do anything remotely like washing, except ritually at Kailas, I was not conscious of body odours. Shigatze had boasted showers in a Han cadre camp. The Ali showers, solar heated, promised to be a treat, but sadly weren't as the water was cold. At least a few layers of grime were removed.

Most afternoons we spent some time hospital visiting. Ali boasts a cottage hospital and we heard two Injies, Alison and Yan were there. 'Injies' (a variation of *feringhi*) appears to be the universal term for caucasians, presumably from the impact of the British Mission Force. Both had come down with hepatitis at Kailas. Alison celebrated her 21st birthday in hospital. Having left home at 15, she had busked her way round Europe, fruit picking here and there, 'done' some of India and then transferred from Katmandu to Lhasa. From there she had set off for West Tibet with 50 yuan and her twelve string guitar. I have to admit that my regular hospital visiting was not simply motivated by Christian altruism, but by the opportunity to play her guitar. She played very well and didn't seem in the least put off by having a drip in her arm. She would have been the utter despair of any British hospital, but here no one seemed too bothered. For a while a Swedish girl shared the room with her, both nurse and free board and lodging. Budget travellers save where and when they can.

For some reason there was often a Public Security man fast asleep on top of a wardrobe in the corridor. The other patient was Jan, a German artist in his late thirties. Based in Spain, he had travelled extensively. He appeared to have become progressively more serious as time went on. He might have provided a foil to Alison's completely carefree approach to life. Utterly irresponsible is how most people would describe her. But hepatitis is not noted for encouraging the light side. I was astonished to be lectured on the wonders of Freemasonry from a Tibetan hospital bed. I couldn't understand why he was so keen to impart these views as it did not look as if we were good candidates for enrolment.

As has already been observed hygiene does not rate highly as a Tibetan virtue. The hospital interior was admittedly a little better than the stagnant pools full of excrement, animal bits and rooting pigs about fifty yards from the door, but roles were reversed and it was Alison who alleviated the boredom by scrubbing the concrete floors. On several days the Indus flooded over to form a small lake which threatend to make her floor cleaning irrelevant.

Few of those who had travelled to Kailas claimed to have enjoyed the experience. Lama Anagarika Govinda, the German-Bolivian who was there in 1949 believed that 'those who have given up comfort and security and the care for their own lives are rewarded by an indescribable feeling of bliss, of supreme happiness'. Maybe Injies were unable to break free from the narrow confines of western intellectual prejudices. Disillusionment was what most felt. They had come so far and for what? Kailas hadn't so much disappointed as failed to inspire. The meanness of the Tibetans, the attempted P.S.B. extortion, the obstructive manager of the guesthouse at Darchen, these were the things that dominated their conversation, not uplifting spiritual experiences or the quest for enlightenment.

Jan, although obviously very ill, had practically been left to die on his circumambulation. It developed more into a crawl, involuntary full length prostration. To the last he was hassled by passing pilgrims for Dalai Lama photos. About the first Tibetan phrase you need to learn is *'Dalai Lama la mei'*. (I haven't any Dalai Lama pictures), unless of course you have come armed with an inexhaustible supply. They are certainly much in demand, but it struck me as a very suspect way of buying one's way round the country. One of the Australians on his way back from Burang, having given the *Parikarama* (the pilgrim circuit of Kailas) a miss, simply dismissed all Tibetans with characteristic Antipodean forthrightness as 'shithouse Lamas'. These tales of woe made me wonder whether going to Kailas was really worthwhile after all. But since the only transport option appeared to be a week or so back to Lhasa no immediate decisions were required.

Meanwhile I explored the surrounding countryside within walking distance, climbing the hills which afforded magnificent views west to the Ladakh mountains. The hill to the west of the town was criss-crossed with shallow trenches, a classic defensive position, but for whom against whom? On the facing hill massive characters *Mao zhuxi wan sui* (long live Chairman Mao) had been scraped out of sand and rocks. The small Buddhist swastika to the right looked like a later addition.

Zop was carrying an impressive library of literature relevant to the area, so I was able to fill in on the view from outside with John F Avedon's 'In Exile From The Land Of Snows', a detailed account of the events of the last thirty years, and in places indescribably sad. If but half of what he reports is true then it is all the more remarkable that pilgrims are now again flocking to the holy places and that life has semblance of normality at all.

9

JOURNEY TO THE
CENTRE OF THE WORLD

'You cannot travel on the Path before you have become the Path itself'.
Gautama Buddha.

I had been spending most of my time with Zop and Peta.
My plans were hanging in the balance. I claimed, and had
half convinced myself, that I was heading home and that my
return was long overdue. They were quite clear that the
purpose of getting this far was to persevere on the road to
Kailas and their enthusiastic conviction inspired me too. I
enjoyed their company and they had assured me they were
happy to share their tent. For a couple of days we
demonstrably failed in our bid to hitch south.

We adopted a dual approach. If the driver was Han or
Uyghur I tried Chinese, if Tibetan then Zop took over. It
wasn't always easy, however, to tell the difference, and a
faulty initial identification was likely to produce a stonewall
response. For the most part anyway it was a case of *'mota
mindu'* (truck don't have) and *'chu chumbu'* (river big), or the
Chinese equivalent. A tour of the truckstops drew a blank
and so we took to the roadside early, but after waiting eight
hours to witness three jeeps pass we rather lost our
enthusiasm for hitching. After several complete changes of
heart and another day failing to get any lifts north towards
Kashgar, we agreed to go for the pilgrim truck south to
Kailas that had been promising to set off for a couple of
days.

By chance we bumped into the driver, having for the first
time changed Sichuan restaurants, and had been informed
they were really leaving in an hour – or two – or three. We
actually climbed onto the ancient Jiefang at 10.30 p.m. but

110

didn't leave until well after midnight, by which time there were twenty-nine people on the back. By the time all were aboard we were practically sitting on the tailgate. We had agreed on 35 yuan for the trip.

Twenty three is my magical number. Like all good obsessions the more I have come to notice it the more significant it has become. It now crops up with almost monotonous regularity. Twenty three is the area code for Tibetan trucks. I was clearly headed in the right direction.

Harrer wisely observed that 'the haste of Europeans has no place in Tibet. We must learn patience if we wished to arrive at the goal'. We didn't leave until well after midnight, and started by lurching off sideways into the Indus, but fortunately didn't fall at the first hurdle. Our resolve was weakening. We suspected the late departure was in order to avoid the traffic police. We bumped along in the dark for an indeterminate length of time, fighting to maintain our positions. We then stopped and lay down on the ground which was cold but bearable. Around 9 a.m. after a brew-up we set off again.

In spite of a little hail it was another beautiful day, with some exquisite scenery. Harrer following the river up towards Gartok described the area thus: 'the scenery was unforgettable. It was the colours that enchanted the eye and I have seldom seen all the hues of a painters palette so harmoniously blended'. I think he rather overdoes it on the range of colours, which tend towards brown and grey. A few fields of stunted barley around Gartok made the scene slightly less desolate.

But packed on the back of the truck was a riot of colour. The Khampas red turbans clashed with purple T-shirts, green and blue Mao hats, aprons of many colours, turquoise earrings, silver daggers, bronze amulets and charm boxes. One of the most impressionable images of Tibet is surely their use of colour. It is bright. It is primary. It is not unlike the native dress, colours and patterns favoured by the Peruvians and Bolivians of the Alto Plano. Is it availability of dyes, the effect of high altitude light, accident, sychronicity, a simplistic childlike nature? We in the West construct our realities on our own experience and tend to assume ours is a

111

greater civilisation, a greater sophistication. For the Tibetans life is much harder. Besides the subtle hues of nature there is little colour in their lives. They have no sumptuous furnishings, little access to possessions, none of the rich trappings of the soft life. Al Koran tells us in 'Bring out the Magic in Your Mind' that you must surround yourself with colour because it has an all important effect on your psyche, on your mind. Colour plays an integral part in Buddhist imagery. White, yellow, red, green and blue symbolise different states of mind and also the Buddhist wisdoms. So colour is fundamental to prayer flags, to their iconography, to their very essence. It adds quality. Brightness is linked to laughter. The Tibetans never seem to stop!

We believe 'red and green should never be seen'. In fact they can be magnificent together. There is a difference, though, between the more muted and faded aprons, the paintings covered by centuries of yak butter lamp grease, and the originals, bright, garish, almost a Tibetan kitsch. Are we frightened of such an unashamed *joi de vivre*?

In China for many years individuality of expression was a luxury the system was not prepared to countenance. This was part economic, as unisex monochrome Mao suits were undoubtedly cheap to produce, but also seemed to reflect an inbuilt distrust of the lighter side of life. Frivolity was out. The Tibetans like many of the other 'Minority' groups didn't appear to have got the message.

This was life at very close quarters and there was no lack of onboard entertainment. Much of the attempted communication was sexual innuendo from the Khampas, emphasised by some graphic gesticulations. The question that exercised them most was whether Peta was Zop's woman, my woman, or belonged to both of us. Understandably as a liberated Tasmanian she didn't greatly appreciate this sexist view. In the wilder parts of Tibet, particularly among the Drogpas, the society is both polyandrous and polygamous. Maybe it just depends on who turns up in your yurt. George Paterson, in his 'Tibetan Journey', an account of his time in the 40's in East Tibet expressed with perhaps just a touch of missionary zeal that, 'the Tibetans are neither

112

completely polygamous nor completely polyandrous, they are completely promiscuous.'

For most of the journey Peta was hijacked up to the front end of the truck where she had marginally more room in return for fighting off the advances of five simultaneous potential suitors. They are nothing if not direct. Not since school days have I been questioned on the size and efficacy of my sexual organs. I'm not sure whether this would have been more or less off-putting if I had shared the language with which to discuss it.

A distinct hierarchy on the truck was evident. We were at the bottom. Next to us were young twin girls, in black traditional dress embroidered with cowrie shells, brightly patterned aprons, intricately patterned sun visors framing their faces, to my eye exceptionally beautiful, but somehow demure and distant. They sat separately from the others, were always the last fed and exuded an almost overwhelming air of sadness. It was speculated that they were 'fallen women' in some sense, though it is not clear how you 'fall' in this society. They were more ignored than ostracised. I would have dearly liked to have known their history. This was indeed true of all our Tibetan travelling companions. There must be so much to tell about life in Tibet since 1950, but the very strong emotions aroused by recent events make objectivity in recording extremely difficult, and the language barrier strictly limits the opportunities for delving behind the scenes.

En route we picked up a tall gangling Japanese, dressed overall in a blue Mao suit and bright yellow anorak, visible from miles off in the arid surroundings. He was on his way from Tsaparang to Kailas, carrying with him a rucksack laden down with large Buddhist tomes, notably the complete poetic works of Milarepa. Like Ekai Kawaguchi, the Japanese monk who reached Kailas in disguise in 1900, he was obviously a dedicated pilgrim, if with a less subtle dress sense.

At Moincer, another bleak collection of mud huts, we stopped for an evening meal, yet more tukba, and acquired a German traveller and a Nepalese Buddhist monk. That made thirty two. Our new addition had adapted well to

Tibetan habits. He simply deposited his impressive bulk on top of Zop who practically disappeared into the bottom of the truck. His gross insensitivity was further confirmed by a French girl we met at Kailas. After travelling with him for three months she had been abandoned, sick and exhausted, in the middle of nowhere, somewhere en route from Tsaparang. It brought to mind the ruthlessness of Sven Hedin, of travellers for whom achieving their own particular goal takes precedence over all other considerations.

From Moincer we drove on until 10 p.m. and then stopped to camp in sight of Kailas with the sun setting over Gurla Mandhatta. The slow murmur of mantras rose to a crescendo of excitement at this first sighting of the Holy Mountain that the Khampa pilgrims from East Tibet had travelled so far to see. Peta noted, 'we were pilgrims of a sort too. To them our journey could only have the same meaning as their own'. In eastern cosmography Kailas has a personality of its own, a vibration or emanation that will impart something of its power even to an agnostic mind. I too felt touched by this. 'I will lift mine eyes unto the hills from whence cometh my help', has always been one of the few lines from many hours of school chapel to have stuck in my mind as holding particular significance. Why I had been drawn to this place was not clear to me, but I knew this was the eve before undertaking a different kind of journey, and not simply because we would mercifully be released from truck travel.

We had not been long camped when a P.S.B. jeep stopped and a heated argument ensued. Surely they weren't going to implement traffic regulations in the middle of the plain. We stayed well out of the way, and fortunately they were soon on their way. The next morning it took a further three hours run to Darchen with changing views of Kailas which stood proud from the surrounding hills, free of cloud, its conical snowcap glistening in the sun. Just short of Darchen we crossed a swift flowing river with a half drowned Jiefang sitting forlornly on the riverbed. This route had been blocked for most of the previous week. There is no other way round.

At Darchen Zop gave the remains of his Indian made

primus stove to our driver. By this stage all three legs had fallen off and the jet had ceased to function, so there was no point in carrying it. I was now at least marginally better prepared, having managed to buy a campermat and a light sleeping bag from one of the Japanese at Ali. But having no stove was a bad start. The truck drivers solve the problem by using big petrol blow torches. Without some such device any cooking is a major undertaking. I don't know exactly what the thermal properties of yak dung are, but they aren't very impressive. Even when reasonably dry we could barely get it to smoulder after a generous application of petrol. The Drogpa often carry a simple bellows (lacba) wrapped around the waist. Boiling a pan of water is more like trying to smelt iron. Timber simply doesn't exist and juniper roots are the best bet for firelighting. The other problem is that even when you have got a fire, because of the altitude water boils at a lowertemperature. As a result nothing really gets cooked properly and similarly nor does it get sterilized.

Why go to Kailas at all? At 22,028 feet it hardly rates with the Himalayan giants, but because it is at the apex of the watershed it stands out on its own. In the ancient Shambala tradition there is an imperial palace set on top of a circular mountain that is named Kailasa. It has long been regarded as the centre of the universe. From within a few miles radius of its foot four of the world's greatest rivers take their source, the Indus, the Sutlej, the Brahmaputra and the Karnali (main tributary of the Ganges).

For the Hindus it is Siva's throne. He sits in eternal paradise, his matted hair falling and flowing out all about him. The Ganges is supposed to emanate from one of these strands. For the Buddhists it is Mount Sumeru or Meru, central peak of the world, Tise, the father mountain and the means to enlightenment. In Tibetan it is known as Kang Rimpoche. In Bon, the animistic and shamanistic religion of old Tibet it is the soul of the country. It assures perpetuity and protection for all Buddhist people.

It is linked stongly with Milarepa the mystical poet, magician, eccentric and hermit, who is a great favourite of the Tibetan people. His unusual qualities appeal greatly to their outlook. Born in 1040 his father died when he was

115

seven years old and an uncle took over their property. Life became very hard for the family and his mother sold her own plot of land to apprentice Milarepa to a black magician. He proved an apt pupil. Using his new found powers he successfully took revenge on the uncle. Immediately afterwards though, he was struck with remorse and started his search for enlightenment. For many years he studied under the tantric master Marpa and thereafter, a sinner who repented of his wild youth, he lived as an extreme ascetic. His hair turned green from eating only nettles, one of the few plants I saw growing around Kailas. This was the scene of his great battle with Naro Bonchung, the champion of the Bon faith. Legend has it that a race was arranged between Milarepa and Naro to be the first to climb Mt Kailas. Naro set off at dawn, mounted on his shamanistic drum. He was making great progress up the mountainside. Meanwhile Milarepa meditated, his followers becoming increasingly agitated as it progressively looked more and more certain they would lose. The stakes were high, for the victor's religion was to be the one to hold sway over all Tibet. At the last moment, by concentrating all his powers, Milarepa flew up to the summit. His opponent in fury dropped his magical drum and crashed to the valley below. Whatever the legends, this is a mountain that has power.

Whether it is intrinsic or lent to it by the sheer weight of the pilgrims' conviction, you cannot help but be affected by it. I had not come overtly looking for enlightenment and thus did not expect to find it. Perhaps this is the best frame of mind in which to stumble on great awareness. I do like mountains, however, and there is something very special about this one.

It has been described as a 'physical manifestation of a metaphysical phenomenon'. On the physical side Sven Hedin likened the Holy mountain to a 'tetrahedron set on a prism', the pilgrims he saw as 'a varied train of shady humanity on the thorny road'. Lying at the hub of the two great Asian civilisations of India and China, it has for centuries attracted pilgrims from great distances. Most of the pilgrims on our truck had come over 1000 miles from East Tibet. At Darchen a packed truck arrived from Burang

116

to the south, bringing Nepalis who had spent several days trekking over the mountain passes.

Over the years it has drawn a bizarre collection of adventurers, explorers and eccentrics. For some like the Victorian Henry Savage Landor it was, if anything, an excuse for 'Boy's Own' heroics gathering material for an adventure best seller. For others like Sven Hedin it was a more serious business. He had a Nietzchean view of exploration as the affirmation of superman in the form of a 'struggle against the impossible'. No prizes for guessing who was going to play superman. Some came simply to shoot game (Speke and Smythe on Shikari in the 1850's) others to map the unknown like the remarkable pundits. They are best known through Rudyard Kipling's 'Kim', where their story, linked to the Great Game with Russia, is told with considerable artistic licence. For sheer fortitude, dogged endurance and commitment their achievements are perhaps the most impressive of all, but have never received the recognition that they deserve. They did, however, have the benefit of natural disguise. Carrying prayer-wheels ingeniously adapted to contain survey instruments, they literally paced thousands of miles through West Tibet, painstakingly keeping a tally on rosaries having not 108 but 100 beads. Even at close quarters their counting could easily be taken for *'Om Mani Padme Hum'*.

Much of this information was gleaned from Zop's travelling library which included a book on Kailas explorers. Among these was Dr Tom Longstaff. I had met him as an old man some twenty years previously on the West coast of Scotland. It was strange, seated below Kailas, to come across a photograph of him at the same spot in 1905. He had just fallen 3000 feet down Gurla Mandhata in an avalanche and then nearly starved to death. (A master of the unassuming understatement this is all dismissed in his own account, 'This My Journey', as another minor mishap.) It is a relief that climbing on Kailas is forbidden. Never ones to let superstition stand in their way, a Briton, Colonel R.C. Wilson climbed to 20,000 feet in 1926. In the same year Hugh Ruttledge and his wife are thought to be the first Europeans to make the circumambulation, taking four days to walk round. Physically it looks quite difficult enough, particularly the 6,000 foot northern face, without having to contend with the spirits as well. Such is the passion for unconquered peaks, however, that I suspect it will not be long before someone has a go at it. Maybe they should bear in mind the cautionary tale from the Rongbuk Monastery below Everest. Before its destruction by Red Guards it is reported climbers discovered that the monks had painted an angry mountain deity, surrounded by demons and what they assumed to be the likeness of Yetis, standing over a speared and naked white climber. Would a similar fate await one so brave or so foolish as to attempt Kailas, arguably a much holier mountain than Everest?

Setting off from Darchen at midday we entered the red valley of Amitabha. Kailas is frequently covered in swirling cloud, hidden from view. We were rewarded with the dazzling ice dome standing proud of its supporting rock pillars outlined against an azure blue sky. The valley itself Lama Govinda described as 'a canyon of red rocks, the structure of which is so architectural in appearance that the pilgrim feels as if he is walking between rows of gigantic temples'. Unlike the desolate plain, here wild life abounds, buzzards and other hawks I could not identify circled overhead, chipmunk-like rodents scurried about. I stopped for a while to watch a whole colony of inquisitive marmots; only half shy, perhaps used to a constant stream of pilgrims. Down the valley tumbled green glacial melt water – after months of the *kai shui* boiled variety from a thermos, I'd forgotten how refreshing the real thing could be. At the riverside we collected juniper roots and yak dung and, by expending a great deal of energy as human bellows, we eventually managed to cook a few noodles. We recuperated in the warm sunlight.

From there we marched until the sun was setting. Above us the rocks towered on either side with waterfalls cascading hundreds of feet down, often only to disappear beneath the scree before emerging as a trickle into the river. On our right, through a narrow defile, the icy West face could be seen, a complex of ledges, ice-falls and extraordinary pinnacles. Although it was far from hospitable, I felt both relieved, not only to be back among mountains and quite extraordinary ones at that, but also a sense of a journey reaching fruition, taking on a shape and a purpose, having meaning and worth. Just past here we camped for the night and caught the incomparable sight of the last pink rays hitting the mountain top. Finally a rosy hue receded into darkness cupped in the valley snaking away north-west towards the source of the Indus.

One might have expected the sleep of the utterly exhausted. Maybe it was too cold despite wearing all the clothes I had with me, layer upon layer. Maybe too much had happened for me to assimilate. My brain was spinning. We talked little, tossed and turned a great deal. Generous though their offer it was clearly not a three person tent. I had a recurring big cat chasing dream – never quite caught, always in danger, always a lurking fear – a burst of pure primitivism. Bruce Chatwin's exposition of theories of the specialist human predator, *dino felis* have since placed this in context: a rational explanation for a deep felt instinct.

I heard most of the pilgrims from the truck pass through, some stopping to shelter behind the rocks for an hour or two. For them no tents. All they carried was a little tsampa. The twin sisters took turns with a large kettle. Even the children kept on doggedly, uncomplaining.

We rose with the sun breaking through freezing mist. Peta had been going slowly the day before, so to even the loads I took the tent. Taking it and setting off ahead on my own was perhaps because subconsciously rebirth was for me an individual rather than a group activity. However, the mantra says, 'I and all sentient beings, until we achieve enlightenment, go for refuge to Buddha, Dharma and *Sangha*.' is a coming together, to share, to pursue the *Dharma* the path. Zop and Peta were my Sangha.

After a couple of weary hours trudging through the mist it suddenly lifted sufficiently to reveal the startling view of the North face. Govinda claims that 'according to the scriptures, it is on this spot that those who are initiated into the rituals and meditations of the respective tantras should perform their devotional practices on the great Mandala of Supreme

119

Bliss'. I wasn't to know this at the time, so instead stole a few photographs of this sight seen by very few Europeans. For me the 'splendid vision' came through the eye rather than from some spiritual awakening. I was in no doubt, however, that I felt a considerable degree of awe, of being dwarfed, of my complete insignificance, and it was probably only my rational western conditioning that held me back from immediate prostration. Would such prostration to the supreme mountain God be a primitive ritual or the only sensible thing to do when confronted with such an imposing and awe-inspiring spectacle? Brought up to a dry Protestantism, part of me envied the perceived devotional excesses of other religions. That I had perhaps somehow been missing out.

Zop and Peta still hadn't appeared. I ventured a little way up towards the col that led to the foot of the sheer ice and rock face. Something other than just the additional physical effort this required held me back. A feeling that it was not meant, that I would be trespassing. I had read that all pilgrims should start on the lowest circuit and that only after twenty-one *Parikaramas* could sufficient merit be acquired to consider the higher middle circuit, and few were supposed to survive that. I obviously had a very long way to go to get off first base.

I returned to the path and carried on over a stone bridge festooned with prayer flags. A narrow wooden plank formed the middle section over which I helped a couple of pilgrim children stoically plodding on behind their mother. At no point is the path so difficult as to require serious scrambling, although in places it is both steep and rocky. Yaks obviously have little trouble in finding their way round the mountain. From the bridge it was a long, slow, breathless climb to an enchanted enclosed valley with little rivulets of fresh melt water gurgling over and under the glistening rocks, a brief splash of wiry green grass, a final recuperation before the last push up to the Dolma La (Tara's pass) at 18,600 feet. This is likened to passing through the gates of death, to be reborn in the valley of Aksobkya to the east. The last few hundred feet certainly felt like the ultimate test. I'll count to fifty I told myself. Usually I would go for a hundred but in this rarefied atmosphere I knew to modify my ambition. By thirty paces this was revised to thirty five. I gasped. My head throbbed. I was passed by some pilgrims who fanned out to gather a rare mountain plant they told me was zuo yao, a medicinal herb. Sadly I never discovered what it was, and lacked the faith later to eat the few sprigs I had been given. A few hundred feet below I had stopped to sunbathe and to give myself an excuse for a rest. At the summit sleet was coming down in a near blizzard. I stopped only long enough to make a quick circumambulation of the summit cairn. It was adorned not only with prayer flags but with a varied collection of banknotes, ingeniously pinned to the rock. These symbolise the irrelevance of material possessions. At several spots lower down I had passed piles of rotting clothing abandoned and strewn over the hillside. I hadn't been tempted to make any such gesture and knew I needed rather more than all the clothing I carried with me.

Reaching the summit should have been the supreme achievment. Maybe knowlege only comes gradually and later. As on so many mountains the weather dictated. This was no place to linger. I was torn between freezing and staying to savour it, to absorb its power, its magical properties; but the sleet forced me on rapidly down past the emerald 'Lake of Mercy' into the valley below.

Reading Chris Bonnington's account of the 1981 Kongur expedition some months later, reminded me of the competitive climbing spirit and the insatiable urge to push on. This is not simply a matter of getting there, wherever that may be, the end of a walk, a summit, for I have always pushed myself hardest when on the hills on my own. What hubris here had forced me on ahead, lungs bursting, blood pounding in my ears? Is enlightenment really to be attained through such self induced suffering?

As I came down, two pilgrims were cheerfully making full length anti-clockwise prostrations up the hill, which suggested they were followers of Bon. Even with wooden blocks to protect hands and knees, the physical pain and exertion must be immense. A 50% survival rate used to be regarded as good for such a pilgrimage.

121

My undoubted feeling of achievement was, however, tinged with more than a little anxiety. No sign of Zop and Peta. I had the tent and the fuel. They had the pegs and the food. After a short debate with my conscience I had greedily eaten the second tin of sardines that I had hoarded all the way from Beijing. After four hours waiting two specks appeared on the skyline and then made their way slowly down the last steep descent. By this stage I had been convinced they had either turned back or succumbed to altitude sickness. The prospect of going back up over the pass had not appealed at all.

While waiting a number of pilgrims had passed. The Parikarama is like a huge human treadmill of a prayer-wheel, wheels within wheels; at this time of year spinning madly. Rebirth must be good for them for I managed to swap nuts and raisins for bread, tea and some dried meat; the latter from a Drogpa accompanied by three girls. We shared only sign language. He had a hard, handsome, inscrutable face. Maybe it was the lack of reference points, but I found his unsheathing a large glistening blade to slice dry meat off a yak bone more than a little disconcerting, and my heart was still pounding away quite enough from the altitude. He looked me over quizzically, I thought threateningly. I gave him more nuts and raisins. Was it a fair exchange? Did it matter? Meanwhile the women looked on with warm interested smiles, squinting out from under intricately patterned visors.

From the time that Zop and Peta finally arrived until it was dark we cooked *tukba*. Firelighting was another exasperating saga requiring the last of our petrol supply. I also had a little kindling that some other pilgrims had left with me having failed themselves to get a fire going; but nonetheless an act of considerable generosity.

After a restless and breathless night we woke to frost on the tent. The sun was not fully up until 10.30 a.m. Hidden in the valley we had to wait for its golden light to creep down the mountainside. Compared with the north side, though, this was lush with a meadow of green grass and Alpine plants. Little streams wove their way in and out of the frozen ponds. From here the going down hill was easier although the river had to be reforded. On the east side lies a small Gompa dedicated to Milarepa, close by the cave where he is reputed to have lived, meditated and composed poetry.

Resting above the roaring river on the last leg down the valley we were passed for the second time by our former truck companions. They hardly stopped to rest, but plodded on, muttering incantations. Most Tibetans make the *Parikarama* three times. The more circumambulations, the greater the merit. For me once was enough. Just walking round and round a mountain, however special, seemed too much like a shortcut. I knew that in any case I was far from ready for it. A family Peta spoke to at Darchen seemed to have taken up permanent residence and had so far been round one hundred and sixty seven times. The level of dedication is almost frightening.

Back at Darchen at last, we should have been flushed with triumph. Instead we found ourselves stranded again. A two person tent for three can be a little cramping. The gooseberry role is not an easy one. Without their offer of shelter though, I could not have undertaken the Kailas trip at all. Tibetans would no doubt have seen a tent as luxury and would not have been bothered with our western concern for personal space. But then there is great encouragement to be had from friends who are foolish enough to share the same discomforts, the same challenges, the same hardships overcome. We were practically out of food, had no fuel and even getting a cup of tea became a major begging expedition. We were, however, rewarded with a double rainbow, which Peta assured us after Kailas was very good karma indeed. We would have liked to have gone south to Lake Manasarovar. That now seemed out of the question.

I had similarly been intrigued by Tsaparang a day's truck ride to the west. This was the capital of the Guge kingdom from about 1100 to 1650 when it was fired and abandoned. The Portugese Jesuit missionary Andrade arrived in

Tsaparang in 1624 and founded the first Christian church in Tibet the following year. At first he found favour with the king who advocated religious toleration. Soon, however, he fell foul of the jealousy of the Lamas and the mission was abandoned. Not long after the kingdom fell apart and the ruins of Tsaparang are all that remain. The wall paintings seen by Govinda in the 1940's were reputed to be superb, the city naturally weathered and decayed but not vandalised. I wondered how it had fared the ravages of the last thirty years. We were never to find out. Being stuck there for a couple of weeks with no food should be left to those following in Sven Hedin's footsteps.

A day doing nothing at Darchen turned out to be very depressing. The English speaking manager of the guesthouse posed as an ally, but his role appeared to be to deny individual travellers access to what little in the way of transport opportunities there were by some ingenious bureaucratic arguments about licensing. Fortunately the next morning we slipped away on a truck that had come in late from Burang.

Behind us careered a light blue Jiefang with five Khampas on the back who whooped with excitement at every bump. Our truck was covered and carried an extended Tibetan family group. The other two passengers were Buddhist nuns from Nepal; the younger, a dull girl, acted as her senior's servant, who thought nothing of physical chastisement for minor misdemeanours.

There were frequent picnic stops and visits to Drogpa settlements for both business and pleasure, the two being inseparable in most Tibetans eyes. In between it was a truck rally with frequent overtaking on the less desperate stretches of road. Our driver carried a two gallon plastic container of *chang* and stopped at two hourly intervals, working his way up from one pint to three, so it was not surprising that our progress became more and more erratic as the day wore on.

The Chinese have been accused of importing large quantities of low grade fire water with which to immobilise Tibetan youth and potential opposition. In Lhasa excessive consumption of *bai jiu* may be as much an expression of despair, a malaise common to many depressed economies and repressed people. Both history and my own limited observations, however, tend to suggest the Tibetans require little persuasion to get uproariously drunk and the Chinese can hardly be blamed for that.

It was pleasant to travel for a change with more women than men and to observe some truck-born family life with a whole range from baby at the breast to a powerful grandmother figure, the matriarchal leader, who smoked cigarettes through an ornate carved wooden cigarette holder.

For much of the journey I was happily distracted by giving my fantasies full reign admiring Pema's classic oval features. Having more Chinese than her parents generation, we were able to converse a little and I ascertained this was for her the first leg of a journey to attend college in Lhasa. She appeared perfectly confident about this step into the unknown at the age of 18.

Her family, she informed me, owned the Jiefang truck in which we were travelling. As an Autonomous Region the position of ownership in Tibet is rather different to that in eastern China. Even when part of a truck team, as most are, the driver has a considerable degree of independence once away from home base and they operate in effect as freelance traders. We were transporting sacks of sugar that had come over the mountains from Nepal to Burang, so she would travel with them all the way to the capital.

My reward in flirtatious recognition of my interest was a plump toungue stuck out, with eyes to match, a traditional Tibetan greeting stolen out of sight of the family. A vision which has travelled with me, a delightful romantic illusion, all the more so for it being so obviously an entirely impractical relationship prospect.

The Khampas in comparison were like a group of little boys, macho, devious, constantly dealing, but full of childish amusement at the world around them. In the afternoon we stopped to eat at a Drogpa camp. Although a storm threatened we delayed until after a rapid rainfall and then, of course, got bogged trying to drive out. After a certain amount of shunting we finally extricated ourselves.

The approach to towing is a little primitive, the preferred method being to take a frayed steel hawser and simply twist it back over itself several times and then hope that when the strain was taken up that the wire would lock. If it didn't, well it was quicker and easier to start again than tieing knots.

It had started to snow and the light had fallen when we finally reached Barr. Earlier rain had turned the road into a quagmire and progress for the last few miles had been painfully slow. Barr is a P.L.A. camp, a walled compound of concrete buildings. These camps act both as staging posts, supply depots for the border troops, and also as wayside inns. We were surprised to find that the reception was quite friendly, but any diversion in this awful barren wilderness must be welcome. The atmosphere was very much more relaxed than one might have expected in a military establishment. It can't have been a popular posting. The tall Uyghur, who appeared to hold some position of authority, informed me he had been there for eight years. I wondered what he had done to deserve this. Famished, we waited impatiently for rice and vegetables to be cooked. The staple diet at these posts is rice, aubergine, green peppers and mutton they buy from passing Drogpas. The Han Chinese think it is a barbaric region. I managed a couple of mouthfuls before rushing out to be violently sick. At least this gave one of the lurking dogs his supper. Fortunately we were allocated a comfortable room with thick warm quilts, and I immediately fell into a deep sleep.

In the morning it was straight out of bed and onto the truck for another day of short dashes and long picnic stops. We followed up the Gar River with the snow clad Karakoram rising steeply from the west side of the valley floor. Well out of Ali we waited for an hour until the sun was setting. The Khampas were dropped off to walk into town. As the light fell we crouched down in the back as the trucks made a mad rush for the last few miles. Over the bridge and we were back in Ali. Cheating the traffic police as always afforded everyone the greatest satisfaction. We'd done it. Mission impossible accomplished. At least we had got back to where we had started.

10

ALI TO KASHGAR

On arrival in Ali we made straight for the guesthouse, but much to our surprise were refused a room. On being pressed, they maintained that Mr Li from foreign affairs had been down in our absence threatening fines if all foreigners were not redirected to the Ali hotel. They weren't very happy about this as they had been doing good business, but they were obviously not in a position to defy the authorities on this matter. The result was that all the foreigners besides the hospital patients had left town, which I suspect was really the intention.

Despite several perceived limitations in the management and appointment, life in the Ali hotel was not all dull. On our last night in town we came back to discover the closest thing to a Saturday night disco in full swing. There was a surprising amount of drinking, a vast crowd of onlookers and a few men dancing with each other to the accompaniment of crackly music and flashing lights. In Kunming my friend Li had smuggled me into a dance-hall which turned out to be an exceptionally tame but bizarre variation on 'Come Dancing'. This looked like a slightly more serious affair with a 'damn the consequences' Wild West atmosphere. The prospect of an evening's dancing in West Tibet was intriguing, but I was feeling ill again and we were due to leave at the crack of dawn, so we left them to their revelry. At least so we initially thought, but in fact the whole hotel was used as a riotous battlefield until the early hours, so we didn't get much sleep anyway. The Chinese are not naturally backward when it comes to being inquisitive. Emboldened by the occasion they regarded our room and persons as public property.

After five days back in Ali we finally came to an arrangement with a Uyghur convoy returning to Kashgar.

For 50 yuan each we were to get a lift the whole way through. As instructed we got up at 7 a.m. and made our way down in the dark to the truck depot. Maybe we were fooled by entering the effects of another time zone, Xinjiang time, more likely we were just being naive. In any event we could not afford to miss this one, so we stood around and stamped our feet until 11 a.m. The convoy consisted of two Mitsubishis and three Russian Maz trucks, the former the creme de la creme of the West China trucking fleet. This was just as well as the next three days were the very hardest trucking. After a month in Tibet I now got my first cab ride, the three of us in the front of one of the Maz's. Two sat next to the driver on the gear box. It would have been fine in the winter, but was a trifle hot for a summer afternoon. The other occupied what at first looked to be the best position, a seat by the window with independent suspension. Unfortunately the freedom of movement was such that the occupant was catapulted up and down, in constant danger of serious head injuries.

Our driver, Achim, aged twenty, was tall suave and Omar Shariff like. Given the state of the vehicle and the nature of the terrain his driving was quite superb. It is certainly no less relevant doing the Aksai Chin run than racing at Monte Carlo, but I did feel his obvious talents should have reached a wider audience. On average they drove 11 or 12 hours a day including repair and rest stops. Their physical stamina was impressive. Every gear change required an act of brute force. On the first day we drove until 10 p.m. with several stops for breakdowns. Our man appeared to be something of a mechanical genius. If the last truck broke down we would always be back within twenty minutes to sort the problem out. This is no country to get stuck on your own.

We stopped for a bowl of noodles at a single, mud and corrugated iron truckstop just outside Rutog which lies on the old caravan trail to Ladakh. Strange to recall that the Jesuit missionary Andrade and his Portuguese lieutenant, Margues, established a second short lived mission here in 1627, it then being a part of the Guge kingdom. Later we were to stop several times by the stony banks of the huge turquoise Pangong lake for photographs. The five drivers

25. Truck race back to Ali.

26. Khampas on Kailas pilgrimage.

27. Yurts near Gartok.

28. Villagers of Kokyar. Taklamakan.

29. Card school. Kashgar.

30. The timber market. Kashgar.

31. Melon feast. Yingkisha.

32. The author leaving China by the back door. Khunjrab.

lined up in front of this impressive backdrop, Karakoram in the distance, and I was enlisted as the official photographer. Such faith was sadly unwarranted, as with a broken meter and no idea of what film they were using, it would, at best, have been inspired guesswork.

As the day wore on I became quite dehydrated, suffering from continual diarrhoea. This wasn't helped by sitting on a hot gearbox for most of the day, or lying out in the burning sun when we broke down. By the time we arrived at Dolma, another mudhut truckstop at 15,000 feet I was feeling very ill. Maybe I also had a touch of altitude sickness. My breathing came in short gasps. Peta put her nursing skills into action and had me propped up in bed. The other four occupants of the dingy room ignored me as best they could, in these parts a gasping neighbour a common irritation, perhaps. After about four hours my breathing finally settled down. This was fortunate as there was no real option to travelling on the next day. I had no desire to join the party at the Ali hospital. Maybe I was being slightly melodramatic, but the thought did cross my mind that this was no place to die. An Israeli the winter before was reputed to have frozen to death on the back of a truck somewhere in this region, but because China doesn't recognise Israel no body was released and the story remains unconfirmed.

We started early in the morning and drove almost non-stop through the Aksai Chin until 11 p.m. Soon after setting off we passed over the border between Tibet and Xinjiang – a cairn by the trackside. This was not much of a border, just the arbitrary legacy of colonial map-makers. Tibet was once a nation state. Greater Tibet encompassed Ladakh, Nepal, Bhutan (land of Bod – the Tibetans), Sikkim, Sikang, most of what is now Qinghai Province, parts of Yunnan and Sichuan.

What does the future now hold for the Tibetan people, their culture and religion? Can they survive and flourish without a national homeland? To see something of Tibet as it was, the advice is usually to visit Ladakh or Dharmsala, the home of the Tibetans in exile. Within the Tibetan Autonomous Region under Chinese control, the process of Sinification, of cultural genocide, may now be irreversible.

Ethnic Tibetans are fast becoming a minority. The unrelenting population pressure from the East of China suggests even the wilderness of the desert areas may eventually suffer the encroachment of Han settlers.

Hope for the immediate future resides with the Tibetans in exile and the manner in which they have exported and revitalised their Buddhist tradition with seats of learning throughout the western world. The Dalai Lama continues to inspire precisely because he offers a very different message to most other leaders in exile. He is consequently much harder to dismiss simply for lacking political legitimacy in the eyes of the Chinese. It was for this reason that the Chinese authorities were so incensed by his Nobel Peace Prize. Sadly their response has been one of pique. In a sense this ageing leadership simply cannot afford to let Tibet go. To do so would be to signal their weakness, the first step to the breakup of the Empire, the passing of the mandate of heaven, that was so nearly wrestled from their grasp in the summer of 1989. Although as a people they are now dispersed, there is something inherent, irrepressible, unmistakable about the Tibetans. Even a Tibetan I met in Switzerland, adopted at an early age and thus removed from his cultural and racial roots had a certain quality, an essence of Tibetan-ness, the ability to laugh from the pit of the stomach, a connection with his emotions, a grounding in a way rarely found in western males.

I had had the good fortune to spend a few short weeks in this still mysterious land at a time of apparent great change and optimism. Subsequent events have dispelled what must now be seen as a naive euphoria about the real and possible rate of radical change in both the way that China and its minority areas are governed. What I have expressed is a personal view through the brief and privileged window that was open to me.

There is a world of difference between the hard-headed Khampas in Tibet, out to survive as best they can, and my retrospective , romantic and rose-coloured view of them. From subsequent study, a circle of friends forged through my travels, an attempt to understand something of the wisdom of the monastic communities in exile, I have tried to make sense of what might simply be seen as many days bumping along in trucks, a walk or two on the wild side, a few half-renovated temples visited. Not all Tibetans have boundless compassion and innate wisdom. Certainly not all Han Chinese are the reverse of this as has been the emotional response of many recent travellers. Committing myself to leaving for China was the first step on the path, a reaching for something out of reach, an idea, a feeling. Was my earlier decision to study Chinese language and culture itself an unconscious choice of a hard path, a remote culture, a very different and difficult language? So the seed for this travel was planted long ago and it has become a tree that is, as it were, still growing.

We can, of course, be wise after the event. I ponder daily on whether I have made of my Tibetan journey a self-fulfilling prophecy. Or was Kailas my Karma? Was I destined to set foot on that path? Tibet and its Buddhist perspective have become a part of me as I continue to write and think and read about them. The process seems interrelated, the time dimension reversible. *Samsara* and *Nirvana* are interdependent, for if there were no confusion there would be no wisdom – cause and effect – and so the wheel turns.

The Aksai Chin is a large tract of wilderness that borders with Indian Kashmir. between 1956 and 1958 the Chinese built a road through the middle of it, the road we were now travelling. The Aksai Chin had been incorporated in British Indian maps at the time of the McMahon Line, though this appears to have heen an agreement with the Lama of a local monastery and never ratified by either Lhasa or Beijing. Border incidents with Indian troops, and it is alleged an Indian attempt to dislodge Chinese troops from a hilltop position, led to a short lived invasion of Kashmir in 1962. The Chinese thereafter withdrew to what they perceived to be the original border and the status quo has since been

131

maintained. Clearly possession is nine-tenths of the law and the Chinese are still there.

Why anyone should want to squabble about such a pathetic prize is a bit of a mystery, although the Chinese are probably in a stronger position to argue strategic necessity as it is the only viable western route between Tibet and Xinjiang. It is one of the most remote and inhospitable places in the world, at over 16,000 feet a vast wilderness of permafrost. Passing through in the middle of August on a clear and sunny afternoon the ground was still frozen solid. Not even the hardiest of Drogpa linger here for more than a few days. For hours in the middle there was just nothing as far as the eye could see. It was a barren landscape of great natural beauty. The foreground was vast, but in the distance snow capped hills with receding glaciers sat above turquoise and aquamarine salt lakes. One can but admire the determination and vision of the Chinese engineers who planned this unnatural line of communication whilst commiserating with the labourers who had to build it. Its major purpose is undoubtedly strategic, a new route through the eastern extremity of the Karakoram. Half the vehicles in any one day were military.

In the late afternoon we halted for half an hour at an abandoned truckstop bearing the weathered inscription *Yaxisun* (Aksai Chin) and *Mao Zhuxi Wan Sui* (Long Life to Chairman Mao). His legacy crops up in the most remote places, not unlike his forerunners, Alexander the Great and Genghis Khan. Maybe someday centuries from now huge Mao statues will reemerge from the desert sands. A mile or so away across the plain an army camp blended into the bleak landscape, surely one of the worst postings imaginable, perhaps even worse than Barr.

In the evening we dropped down beside the Karakax river, the glacial waters that run down to give life to the old silk road cities and then disappears into the Taklamakan desert. We stopped to eat at Dahong Lintan and finally reached Zaidulla (Shahidulla) by nightfall. Despite the long day I felt much better again, possibly because I had descended below 12,000 feet for the first time in five weeks. I had been told you are supposed to feel like superman after descending from long periods at high altitudes, so maybe I hadn't fully recovered afterall. The by now routine bowl of noodles at the end of the day was most welcome. Cutting and the Roosevelts travelling through here in 1925 did rather better by bringing their own supplies. 'Before dinner we managed some succesful cocktails of Scotch whisky, sloe gin, juice of preserved pears, and a dash of cherry brandy', and that was only an aperitif we are led to believe. Earlier generations of travellers were obviously better organised and had much harder heads.

Colonel Alexander Gardiner, a strange figure taken to wearing full tartan Indian uniform in later life, probably crossed the Karakoram and the Kunlun in the 1830's on his many wanderings with brigands. His perceived eccentricity (going native), obvious tendency to embroider an already extraordinary history, and the extreme confusion surrounding his claimed journeys sadly means that this cannot be verified. The first Europeans recorded as having done so are the German Schlagintweit brothers travelling in 1856. However they wrote at such length and with so little humour that their account has never been translated into English and has been read by remarkably few Germans. Their achievements have thus remained firmly rooted in obscurity.

The prospect of opening up trade to Yarkand (now Shache) fascinated a whole generation of explorers, adventurers and traders from the time of Moorcroft's travels in the 1820's. He had heard rumours not only of a pass but a road from Rutog to Kotan (Hetian). If this did indeed exist as a road at this date then it was the route we had just travelled. Later travellers, however, make no mention of a road, concentrating on the impossibility of the terrain. The man who really forced the route was Johnson of the Indian survey who for many years after 1864 held the altitude record reaching 23,000 feet surveying in the Karakoram. On this occasion he journeyed on three days beyond the pass towards Yarkand, safe in the knowledge that unknown to the British authorities the Maharaja of Kashmir had established a garrison at Shahidulla. I don't know whether this has been used as a precedent in relation to the Chinese-Indian border

133

dispute. The following year Johnson followed east up the Changchenmo valley and then struck north over the Aksai Chin reaching the Karakash river within three weeks. In 1868 both Robert Shaw, Younghusband's uncle, and his rival George Hayward spent several weeks stuck at Shahidulla awaiting permission from Yakub Beg, the Moslem ruler of what was then known as Altyn Shahr, the Land of Six Cities, to cross the Kunlun to Yarkand. For a while after their return from Eastern Turkestan it was thought that the Karakoram-Kunlun route could provide a channel for trade across the mountains, as did Andrew Dalgleish, an enterprising Scots merchant, who had arrived in Yarkand in 1874 shortly after the British mission to Kashgar lead by Forsyth. By the time of his death, hacked to pieces by his former companion Daud Mohammed in 1888, the route had come to be recognised for what it really was, a death trap for all but the most fortunate of travellers.

The next morning it was straight from bed and onto the truck at first light, from the world of dreams to the fantastic reality of the passes through the Kunlun mountains. After Mazar we churned and growled our way up a glacial stream bed, a perfect living geography lesson. Sadly, though, the view from the top of the highest pass was obscured. We had hoped to see back towards K2, though I doubt there is intervisibility .

The second pass was both impressive and terrifying. The way was of course rough and single track. The higher we climbed the more moist and slippery it became. Perched in the window seat I had an almost vertical view of the 4,000 feet drop everytime we went round a hairpin bend. On the far side we met a whole convoy of P.L.A. Jiefangs inching their way uphill. Our attempts to pass them where there seemed quite insufficient room to do so, led to us rapidly abandoning our vehicle. Achim looked faintly askance at such faintheartedness and squeezed past with stones cascading away down into the abyss. The sort of spot that Captain Deasy, another intrepid explorer at the end of the century, describes with masterly understatement as 'a nasty corner for camels' on a caption of a photograph of camels that appear to be perched on a near vertical cliff face.

Round and down, down and round, round and down we went. Dizzily we emerged onto another plain, but this time at a sensible 4000 feet. We passed our first tree since Shigatze and entered a completely new topography, hot desert with greenery only where the mountain water had been channelled. After several days in the wilderness we had also entered a new and different culture. Remember we were still in China, but this is what used to be known as Chinese Turkestan or Sinkiang. The people speak a variety of Turkic languages and use a Turkic script. The religion is Islam, but the women are unveiled and take an open and active part in town and village life. The impact of Chinese communism is only immediately apparent in the ubiquitous Mao hats.

At Kokyar, the first village of any appreciable size we ground to a halt. Achim discovered we had fractured a fuel line. Half the village gathered to observe us, and much to our delight we were invited into one of the houses where, seated on richly coloured rugs and cushions, we were treated to a feast of nuts and sweets, addictive sugar tea, apricot kernels and raisins, followed by rice and mutton. Outside they had not only grapes but huge pumpkins trained to grow down the trellised arches. After the hardships of the last few weeks this village was the closest thing to civilisation we had seen in a long time, a most encouraging introduction to Xinjiang.

Sir Aurel Stein, who following on from Sven Hedin made remarkable archaeological discoveries in the lost cities of the Silk Road in the Taklamakan desert, visited Kokyar at the beginning of the century. He too found it a peaceful small oasis. Unable to resist any opportunity for accumulating knowledge, he even took cranial measurements of the little known local population, the Pakhpo. Despite this he received great hospitality. Maybe it was their descendants who treated us with similar generosity.

A tractor and trailor load of Han Chinese on their way back to an oilfield nearby were keen that we should accompany them. This was an intriguing prospect. We had not been used to a great deal of hospitality of late, but we felt an oilfield was not the sort of place the P.S.B. would appreciate us visiting. We were also reluctant to jeopardise what we thought was a lift right through to Kashgar. Sadly we declined and climbed back on board the Maz. Only half a mile down the road we stopped opposite the market. After some heated negotiations we, along with the Han Chinese passengers, were transferred to a battered old Jiefang. Achim explained that by this method we would be able to avoid the roadblock. Otherwise they would be fined 30 yuan for each passenger. To demonstrate his good faith he agreed to pay the 4 yuan difference. It all looked very dubious, but we didn't appear to have much option. We were sorry to see the convoy drive off without us.

Our fears were almost immediately realised. We drove off down the road for a few yards, the truck jerking uncontrollably. The lights were so dim the road ahead was near invisible. After half a mile we stopped and our driver stated that the vehicle was incapable of further progress. Despite our objections and an anxious chorus from the Chinese on the back he slipped out of the cab and off into the bushes. After a long wait he reappeared, started the truck, and drove again in the dark back to the market place, suggesting that we should go and stay in a guesthouse for the night. Further argument ensued and again he slipped away into the night. By this stage the Chinese were becoming very excitable. We thought this was a time to demonstrate superior philosophical detachment and proceeded to gorge ourselves on slices of melon that were still on sale at this late hour at a market stall. After another hour wondering what we ought to do next, Achim and one of the other convoy drivers suddenly reappeared, stating that one of their trucks had been driven off the road by an oncoming P.L.A. convoy and that the axle was broken. They were looking for reinforcements to attempt a salvage operation. We in turn explained our predicament and our grave dissatisfaction with our new driver. Achim eventually found him, we remounted and set off. Lo and behold, there was nothing wrong with his truck afterall. Twenty kilometres down the road the Maz lay slewed over into the desert sand. It wasn't going anywhere for the time being, so on we went.

At some stage in the early hours of the morning we passed the road block I had been warned of way back in Shigatze. Across the track lay a telegraph pole. A few yards away were two policemen asleep on a double sleeping platform with an awning above them. We stopped and blew our horn. Peta and I, hearts pounding in the front, pulled down our Mao caps. The rest crouched down in the back. One of the policemen sleepily rose from his bed wearing only a pair of underpants. To shouts from our driver he stumbled over to lift the pole, and with no further inspection we were through. The last eleven kilometres into Yecheng were metalled. First trees, now metalled road, what next we wondered?

Spare a thought for our Han fellow travellers. Already they had sampled the rigours of travel in Tibet, for many of them a singularly disquieting experience. A couple of thousand miles from home in a largely hostile environment, they had good reason to be anxious of P.S.B. checkpoints. For them the penalties for infringements are considerably more severe than anything meted out to foreigners, despite the fact that in Chinese terms the foreigners have no real justification for being in such situations in the first place.

If they feared the Tibetans and the P.S.B., they appeared to fear the Uyghurs even more. The Han Chinese are not a naturally violent people. My observations of Uyghur culture over the next few days were to suggest that they are in a completely different category. They are extremely volatile. Life has a sharp edge. Fanaticism is not far under the skin. Street fights are common, the level of aggression among children is quite marked.

There have been a few great Chinese travellers, like the Buddhist pilgrim Hsuan Tsang. But he was primarily a pilgrim with a purpose, the collection of Buddhist scriptures from India. Certainly he wasn't travelling for the fun of it. The spirit of adventure, the restless wanderings of western explorers, is not an essential part of their culture. None of them had been reared on Newby, Kerouac or Fleming. By choice these Han wouldn't have been where they were. For us the hardships of the road had been our own choice. If 'wanderlust' simply exposes you to hardship and places you in the hands of unscrupulous minority knaves, barbarians no less, then they wanted nothing of it.

The attitude of the authorities would appear to be that

137

either you are travelling on official business, in which case you will have a fistful of papers to justify your journey, or you must be up to no good. Unauthorised travel between Tibet and Xinjiang is not encouraged. Our companions definitely came into the latter category of travellers, and consequently it was easy for our Uyghur driver to put on the squeeze.

In Yecheng at last the driver stopped by a noodle restaurant and indicated that we should now eat. We thought we should find somewhere to stay for what was left of the night yet another argument. He held the keys. So in we went to an unattractive scene, not because of the dirt, by Tibetan standards it was almost clean, but from the tangible atmosphere of hostility. As had happened so often in Tibet, we were the last to be served. As soon as we had got our bowls our driver told us we were now going again. This seemed a bit rough since we had waited several hours for him. A fight was imminent. Back out again to the truck. Peta announced she had had enough mucking about and that she was going to find a place to stay for the night above the restaurant. Even the driver seemed to think this was not a good idea. It subsequently turned out to be the local brothel. I wanted to go on to the bus station to have the best possible chance of getting transport on to Kashgar. I was also having a sudden burst of paranoia about how effective my 'travel permit' was likely to be in convincing the authorities. Our truck convoy would have to go back to salvage the damaged vehicle, so they were unlikely to travel on to Kashgar for a day or two at least. Zop was caught in the middle. He was also for going on to the bus station, but felt this was hardly the situation in which to leave Peta. Luggage was taken off the truck and put back on again several times. An ineffective babble of complaints from the Han, but for the most part *sotto voce*, (if this is possible in Chinese) so that no one would be picked out for retribution. Finally I set off down the road with one of the Han, wondering whether I would see Zop and Peta again. It had hardly been an auspicious leavetaking. I managed to get a bed for the remainder of the night, three hours, at the bus station. I would have done better without, as three hours was quite long enough for a serious bedbug attack.

Yecheng, formerly Kargilik and once famous for its silk, has been transformed into a modern (concrete) Chinese city. Although the days of the Silk Road are long since gone, it still has an important role as a communications centre. The bus station was a hive of activity. Huge crowds literally fought their way onto each bus. Projected times of departure were more in hope than expectation. Despite having bought a ticket I had no seat, indeed counted myself lucky to have got onto a bus at all, and had to stand most of the eight hours to Kashgar. When I say that the bus was packed, I mean literally that all available space was occupied. For the first leg I had one third of one step down to the door. On the plus side the road is for the most part metalled but the scenery is at best unremarkable, a couple of hundred miles of featureless desert. En route we stopped at Yarkand and Yingkisha, but besides a tantalising peep at the older parts of these towns as we drove through the outskirts there was little to see in the centres except standard concrete architecture.

In Lhasa one of the odd pieces of traveller's lore that I had picked up was that the best place to stay in Kashgar was the 'Seaman's Mission'. This seemed highly improbable advice as Kashgar is about as far from the sea as you can get. However, bearing this in mind, I asked directions to what I assumed must be a mythical organisation. Not so, it is not a 'Seaman's Mission', but the *'Se Man Bingguan'* (Colourful Hotel). The old part of the hotel was originally the Russian Consulate. The residence of the British Consul, the Idi Bagh, is now also an hotel, but less grand than the Se Man. Since schooldays and the effects of my grandfather's misguided attempts at character formation, I haven't been over enthusiastic about cold showers, but on this occasion it was clearly the 'civilisation' component of the hotel which advertised itself as 'Joint Building Hotil-With Civilisation'.

11

HAT CITY

Xinjiang, New Dominion, has two major cities, Urumqi, the capital, now a vast industrial complex, and Kashgar in the west, still largely a traditional oasis where the Han influence is less pronounced. Kashgar has a ring to it, a promise of mystery, in part the magnet that had led me the long way round through Tibet. The present day city is not the Cascar of Marco Polo which was destroyed at the end of the Sixteenth Century. It's ruins, Eski Sharh, lie fifteen miles east. The Kashgar I found, however, was far from lacking in atmosphere and romance. With 14 million, Xinjiang is after Tibet the most sparsely populated region. The Uyghurs, ethnically close to the Uzbeks in the Soviet Union, remain the largest group, but only just, with 46%. The Han now account for almost 40%, either in garrisons. as settlers, or a large number of permanently relocated 'criminal elements' making the province into a Chinese version of Siberia. There are also an appreciable number of Kirghiz, Tadjik and Tungans, and there have been several emigrations of Russians. The latter date back to the middle of the last century when the Old Ritualists (*Rasholniki*) fled Tsarist repression. There have since been waves of defeated White Russians, followed by a number of Kazaks and others fleeing collectivisation.

In 1949 when the population stood at 4 million the Han constituted less than 10%. Socially there is little intermingling, intermarriage is rare, and few of the governing Chinese have bothered to learn the local language. Segregation is also a feature of education and is further accentuated in separate canteens as the Islamic diet is irreconcilable with the Chinese taste for pork. There is little love lost between the two groups. If anything, the Uyghurs have more in common with their fellow Muslims across the Soviet border.

Until the Revolution, Chinese control over the region was often tenuous, although at periods when the Empire was strong tribute was regularly sent to the east. Surrounded by the Tien Shan to the north, Pamirs to the west, and Karakoram and Kunlun to the south, it has had to rely on two difficult caravan routes north and south of the Tarim Basin. Thus natural barriers on three sides have mitigated against invasion and absorption, but the distance from Chinese control in the east has meant long periods of semi-independence. The Uyghurs and Tungans have proved a troublesome headache for the Empire, Nationalists and Communists alike. In 1930, for instance, the ruling warlord invited Russian troops in to quell a rebellion, and Russian influence remained strong up until 1942 as they took advantage of the Nationalists' preoccupation with both the Japanese and the Communists. As elsewhere, the Cultural Revolution has left lasting antagonisms, and as recently as 1981 a brief uprising near Kashgar was bloodily suppressed by the P.L.A.

Chinese influence in the area is not a recent feature. There is a long history of contact with Han China, and some of the oldest remains of its civilisation have been unearthed at Khotan and Turfan. Ptolemy is reported as claiming Tashkurgan to the south of Kashgar as the extreme western point of the Chinese Empire and the same situation pertains today.

My first priority in Kashgar was to re-establish contact with the outside world. Before leaving Kaifeng I had given my cousin Liz the address of the Kashi Binguan (Kashgar Hotel). I had also sent a couple of address labels home. As I had arrived several weeks later than I had expected I was sure there would be mail awaiting me. Consequently I made my way out to the hotel, a long walk across to the east side of town. The counter clerk assured me there was no mail for foreigners. *"Mei you, Mei you"*. I didn't believe him. I didn't want to. He countered that the only mail for a foreigner had been one letter for a Japanese two months previously. My enquiries became more heated, his denials similarly so. I thought of trying the direct approach climb over the counter and rummage about, but I wouldn't have known where to start. Defeated and dejected I left muttering to myself. Uncertain of my ground here I was not sure whether to invoke the wrath of Allah, or launch an attack on the evil of obstructing the development of efficiency and the Four Modernisations.

The Abakh Hoja Tomb, a short donkey cart ride out to the east, restored my humour slightly. A variation on the 'seen one temple seen them all' principle, this was a very different scene to the Buddhist and Daoist temples I had so far investigated. As is no doubt intended, the greens and blues of the exquisite tile work give an air of repose and tranquility the art and colour sense of Islam a world apart. I was intrigued by the large cemetry at the back, a forest of burnt earth tombs, like miniature elongated mosques, casting a maze of fantastic shadows.

Back into town to book phone calls home, I waited for four hours but failed to get through. It is difficult to determine whether the problem arises at the counter or down the line. Certainly it is the counter operator who has to bear the brunt of the outbursts from angry foreigners who want immediate connections to countries they haven't heard of, conducting their enquiries in unintelligible languages. Add to this the time factor, not simply international, but the Xinjiang time–Beijing time credibility gap, and it is something of a miracle that connections are made at all. It certainly hadn't occured to me that you might be able to telephone from Kashgar until I overheard discussions of expected waiting times.

If you have nothing better to do the telephone hall is always a good meeting place. Next door in the Post Office I checked Poste Restante and was depressed to find that half my travelling companions had piles of mail waiting, but none for me here either.

The next day I finally got through after only an hour and a half. There is a certain satisfaction to waking your mother at 7 a.m. with such a call. "Hello Mum, it's Rod. I'm calling from Kashgar." This most welcome contact redressed the balance for the lack of mail, although it was impossible to begin to condense into a few short words all that I had done, felt and thought since Kaifeng a lifetime or two ago.

Layers of grime you take for granted, accept as a natural state in Tibet. But in Kashgar a single shower didn't feel like sufficient cleansing. So like a cowboy who has ridden into town from the Wild West I took myself to a barber shop to 'get them whiskers off'. One yuan for haircut and shave, the foam applied by a small boy, the shave deftly executed with a cut throat razor, the operation topped off with an eyebrow massage. Why bother to shave yourself when you can get such a magnificent service for next to nothing?

Across the street from the barbers I found a shop where musical instruments were made and repaired. The craftsman sat before a jumble of pieces of wood, tools and half finished instruments. His creations ranged from five stringed *Rawops* to *Tampas* to various kinds of *Sass*. There was also a large three stringed instrument, their equivalent of a bass guitar. After the musical desert of China and Tibet it was a joy to be back among people for whom the sheer pleasure of spontaneous musical creation is an important part of everyday life.

A few days before my arrival they had had the first major religious and musical festival that had been permitted since the Revolution reached Kashgar. For three days and nights there had been non-stop live music from the top of the Idi Kah Mosque in the centre of town.

A massive reinforced concrete statue of Mao dominates the centre of the Chinese city. Attempts to destroy it are believed to have been abandoned for fear of dynamiting not only Mao but many of the surrounding buildings. The same uniform Han influence, the concrete administrative buildings, the broad metalled streets, have arrived here too, but I warmed to the rich colours, the confusing mud streets and houses of the old city, above all the bazaar teeming with activity. The predominant fashion for girls appeared to be layers of brightly coloured silks and muslins, a see-through Indian restaurant wallpaper design being most favoured.

Kashgar is hat city. They come in all shapes and sizes, from short and tall fur rimmed ones to intricately embroidered Muslim skull caps. Flat caps are also much favoured by the Uyghurs in preference to Mao hats giving the strange sensation of being surrounded by an army of stable boys. This is heightened because this is very much a male dominated society where boys as young as three and four are out on the street in groups, flat hats at jaunty angles, squatting down to play cards. The impression of adulthood is slightly ruined by puddles of urine expelled through their split crotch trousers. A whole section of the bazaar is devoted to hats. Hanging at the front of one of these stalls was a magnificent snow leopard skin. No wonder it is prized for its beauty, but its open display in the market place suggests protection controls for this threatened species are not very effective. I had seen another snow leopard pelt of lesser quality being bartered by a Khampa in the Barkhor in Lhasa.

Kashgar is also famous for its engraved ornamental knives. These are both very finely worked and very cheap, but I couldn't see any practical use for most of them and suspected that they would be a liability travelling, so forwent a knife collection. The rug sellers passed the day playing western chess, rather than Chinese. Rug experts assured me Kashgar rugs were not up to much compared with those from Bokhara, Samarkhand, etc. Anyway rugs are even more difficult to carry than knives.

For instant gratification, though, the fruits in the bazaar take some beating; the most delicious yellow figs, the most juicy and succulent honey melons, water melons, and many others I could not name. I guzzled some ice-cream, no doubt a serious health hazard, but this was the opportunity to make up for all the austerity and privations of the last few weeks. If needs be let the School of Tropical Medicine examine the ravages on my return, I rashly thought. I had been strongly conditioned by my bacteriologist grandfather who took a dim view of ice-cream and carried an obsession about cleanliness to the extreme of demanding my father sterilise his sword before using it to cut his wedding cake.

Across the road from the Seman Binguan was a Sichuan restaurant producing excellent food, and the proprietors were amenable to suggested improvisations in the kitchen. I offered to write out a Chinese-English menu for them, but at first they didn't seem terribly impressed. I had been sure this was a ticket to at least one free meal, as well as good *guanxi*. I was happy to note that the menu was soon being put to good use, but unfortunately I did not stay long enough to cash in on the *guanxi*.

An interesting variation on the cooking here is that, doubtless because of the Muslim influence, even in most Han restaurants, there is no pork. Mutton and beef are the prinicipal meats, noodles, rice and a variety of breads are all available. Noodles are hand rolled in long thick noose shaped snakes. Excellent shashlik are sold on the street.

Much of my time in Kashgar was whiled away at 'Gera's', a most surprising establishment. Gera, in his early twenties, was half Russian, half Uyghur. If Xinjiang is an Autonomous Economic Region, then he is a prime example of the individual entreprenuerial activity that is supposed to be encouraged. Using a modicum of English and a keen appraisal of the needs of travelling foreigners he had set up the ideal business, a cafe outside the hotel, but requiring no early morning expeditions through back alleys to get back to your bed, a relaxed atmosphere to sit and read, write, or play chess, with supplies of coffee, omelettes, icecream, even real whisky if you could afford the prices. All this with tasteful cane furniture and a cassette player was almost too good to be true. In a sense it performed the function for us that the British Consulate (now also an hotel) had done for Peter Fleming after his voyage through the Gobi and Taklamakan deserts with the Swiss adventurer Kini Maillart in 1935. It offered an oasis of tranquility and repose, a chance to recuperate. You don't realise how much you need to until you actually stop.

The traffic was very much two way. Gera thirsted for information and ideas from the West. In return we were keen to advise him on how best to cater to our requirements.

At the time it appeared it also met with the tacit approval of the authorities as a suitable venue for meeting travellers' needs without having them roaming about all over town, either risking incidents or witnesing things they might prefer hidden. I would be very surprised to hear if it was still in operation.

On my second night in town a veritable party got under way at the cafe with the American climbing party from K2 we had met very briefly at Mazar and the Australian and Americans who had passed through Ali. The latter had dropped off at Mazar and set off in search of the former. They met a couple of days short of K2 when the K2 team were retreating. Beaten back by bad weather before they reached the summit, the rivers were already so high on their return that they only managed to cross with difficulty on the back of camels. To add to their reunion celebrations I had one as well. Don, Bill and Denise were already in town. Halfway through the evening Zop and Peta appeared. It was only a day's travelling since we separated at Yecheng, but we fell on each other like long lost friends, in part a reflexion on the unsatisfactory nature of our earlier leave taking.

The Sunday market is the most important event of the week in Kashgar. Traditionally the centre of economic life, it is now perhaps more of an alternative black economy in comparison with the state controlled enterprises. The atmosphere was suitably biblical. I saw large men with magnificent beards and any one of the many available hat styles perching incongruously on tiny donkeys, and all manner of livestock, even three rather sad looking Kirghiz Bactrian camels. The largest of these, at the best of times unattractive animals, looked grossly syphilitic, being practically noseless. A Japanese traveller was rumoured recently to have bought one to ride to the border. One can only hope it was not from this particular stable.

146

12

LEAVING CHINA BY THE
BACK DOOR

For an early morning send off from Kashgar I acquired the welcome services of Robert, an American chiropracter. I was drinking beer one evening on the hotel patio and must have been looking insufficiently relaxed. I have an idiosyncratic tendency to exercise my neck emitting from time to time alarming clicks. Mostly I am blissfully unaware of this. He suddenly asked, "Would you like your neck sorted out?" I am naturally a bit apprehensive about gratuitous offers of manipulation, but after discussing the matter concluded he knew what he was up to. His initial visual diagnosis was certainly quite accurate, whereas for him he suggested it would be a good opportunity to keep his hand in (or hands, as the case may be). The weeks of truck travel in Tibet couldn't have done my spine any good. I'm sure being rearranged before the Chinese bus experience was the best possible start to the next journey. I must remember on my next trip to enlist the services of a personal masseur.

The bus station was the usual scene of utter chaos. One bus south had already been postponed the day before, so for a start the number of tickets sold was bound to exceed the number of seats available on one bus. This is always assuming, unwisely I am sure, that the tickets sold would correspond to bus seats anyway. I had sufficient experience of China travel by this stage to know that a ticket did not necessarily equate to a seat. A novelty here for me, though, was having to weigh in our baggage, however meagre. This then had to be paid for by weight and a receipt was issued, which in turn we were required to hand to the English speaking bus company representative. She then supervised the loading of the luggage onto a Dong Feng truck (China's newest Izuzu copy) sitting next to our bus.

We finally got away by 11 a.m. with a full complement of twenty-eight for the border and a further eight extra passengers squatting with their packs in the aisle destined for the Karakhol lakes. Boarding Chinese buses is in one sense organised on democratic principals. Tickets are numbered not for seats after all they may be broken, removed, never have existed in the first place but by the order in which they are sold. You mount the bus according to your number and then have to do some quick thinking in relation to the available options. With less places remaining obviously the choice is more limited, but it is also more dificult. Holding one of the last numbered tickets I got a back window seat. Naively, after Tibetan trucks I thought this particular journey would be a 'doddle'. The Karakoram highway had only officially opened on May 1st. Surely the going would be reasonable.

I was, of course, sadly mistaken. Another mistranslation perhaps, or does 'open' have a different connotation in Chinese in relation to roads? From the moment we left Kashgar the road got progressively worse, and worse, and worse.

The first day's run was for the most part flat (except the unmetalled road surface), hot, dusty and boring, unless you find unchanging stony desert scenery of interest. I was fortunate to find Ben and Una seated next to me, to cultivate and nourish the inner vision. It was through 'Gera's' that I first met them. One of my two remaining operable tapes was 'Moving Hearts Live', the Irish traditional/rock band. There was no surer way of attracting a discerning Dublin girl's attention than giving Moving Hearts their first air time in Kashgar. If the British have been noted for exporting their eccentrics over the years, then Ben fitted firmly in this tradition. Tall, slim almost to emaciation, with close cropped fair hair, much travelled in India, he was something of a hat fanatic long before he ever reached Kashgar. His favoured headgear at this juncture might best be described as of the North African fez family. After a field day in the Kashgar bazaar, half his slim pack carried an eclectic collection of Xinjiang fashions. A natural raconteur, he kept us in stitches to counteract the violent bumping of the bus.

A self-made man in fruit machines, he had made sufficient fortune to travel while having the misfortune to have experienced college life at Oxford, not as a student, but as a servicer of refectory gaming machines. This had given him a very jaundiced view of the elitism, interests and social mannerisms of this privileged class. This inevitably created an experiential credibility gap between him and Una and myself.

She was small, dark, dynamic, green eyed, at once both severe and homely, irresistible. An ex Dublin student of classics and Irish, another interesting link in the linguistic chain, she was naturally endowed with the gift of the gab. At first these differences in experience were of no great moment, but as the days passed they were to intrude to a greater extent.

One mid-morning stop was made for a noodle stall bunfight, a major challenge to the travellers' digestion so early in the day. Perhaps there is something to be said for not eating at all on the road, as in Tibet. En route we passed a gallant mounted Japanese, looking to all intents and purposes as if he had escaped from the film set of a Japanese martial epic. The European stereotype of the Japanese is just that – a stereotype. Besides the reciprocally held view that they/we all look alike, we tend to think of them as identical high technology industrial wage slaves, tied to their computers, company cars, company flats, company way of life. The individual Japanese travellers I met were almost invariably the antithesis of this: individualistic, non-conformist, enterprising and courageous travellers. They also often brought the contemplative, philosophical aspect to the fore that was for the most part so conspiciously lacking among the brasher Westerners. Although they do enjoy some advantages, like easier disguise and a head start with the written language, it should not be forgotten that the Japanese are not exactly well liked in China.

By nightfall we arrived at Bulukou. Progress had been painful and slow. I felt ill, but managed to down some rice and vegetables. Quarters for the night (for most of us) were the concrete floor of a large room for which 3 yuan a head was demanded. We at least enjoyed the limited satisfaction

149

of my being buried under some blankets, so saving ourselves a miserly three yuan. At 76 yuan for the trip, which most had had to pay in FEC, this was a very expensive bus journey for the distance and resources provided, which only goes to show that the Chinese are no fools in relation to the laws of supply and demand.

The eight extras were headed for the lake below Kongur that we would pass on the way. Two young Germans believed they would be able to make the lake and back to Kashgar for the flight to Urumqi within two days. They should have known it is wildly overambitious to plan any return journey in China to take only two days. Not only were they going to lose over two hundred yuan each for the airfare, but would be very lucky to pick up another flight within a week. So far they had stood in the aisle of the ponderously lurching bus for a long day and we still looked to be several hours short of the lake. No sign at this stage of the luggage truck.

Off we set in the morning at 7.30. No breakfast. The air already warming. Progress was again slow and further interrupted by a couple of major breakdowns and constant stops for water for a leaking radiator. In this arid landscape water is a precious and scarce commodity, at least where and when you want it. To get round this problem the driver ingeniously adapted a shredded inner tube into a huge gourd which was then lashed by the doorway, sloshing its contents back and forth.

The road between Bulukou and Tashkurgan ranks along with West Tibet as one of the worst roads in China, certainly for a major trunk road. In comparison with the magnificent engineering feat of the Khunjrab Pass on the Pakistan side, with miles of metalled road through huge rockfalls, towering cliffs, receding glaciers and rushing mountain streams in spate, this road is a very haphazard affair indeed.

There are virtually no bridges or culverts. The sand and gravel has simply been bulldozed up into an uneven ridge which washes out every time a stream fills up. This coupled with recent attempts to rectify the situation with some basic engineering has lead to parallel roads, one under construction, the other lurching from washout to washout in a series of sickening jolts. I suppose we could at least claim to have seen the Karakoram highway much of the way on the Chinese side, even if we weren't actually travelling on it. On a couple of occasions we all had to dismount for the bus to negotiate particularly bad washouts.

It seems strange the Chinese should have contributed to building the Khunjrab Pass whilst paying so little attention to the Kashgar-Tashkurgan road on their own side of the border. Particularly as over four hundred Chinese lost their lives labouring on the Pakistani side.

We gradually gained height, reaching almost to the snow line on the pass that took us past the lake. For once no clear blue sky. Across the lake and mirrored in it as they emerged from the cloud were the two mighty and spectacular peaks of Kongur and Mustagh Ata. There was, however, no sign of habitation. In view of the transport difficulties so far, the Germans, perhaps wisely, decided they would not abandon ship at this stage even if the ship was foundering.

Pakistani buses possibly have even less room than Chinese, but there the Chinese credit balance ends. The Pakistani buses are more like travelling artworks with doors back and front, windows that wind all the way up, using either new Nissans or Bedford chassis. Where Pakistani buses have shiny chrome, Chinese buses have shiny metal, the paintwork long ago worn off, most of this onto passenger's clothing as they groped for purchase on the buses' erratic journeying. Outside, the paintwork, or lack of it, is mirrored with faded, barely distinguishable notice boards at Khunjrab (Hongqilafu) and contrast with a brisk military efficiency and new lick of paint at the Pakistani Frontier Force security checkpoints.

By 6 p.m. we had reached Tashkurgan, principal town of the Tadjik Autonomous District. It promised to be an exotic spot, but all we saw of it was yet another truckstop and a wide tree-lined avenue. The driver appeared to be keen for us to stay the night at the truckstop, but after some standard noodle fare and then having slipped down the road for a more substantial meal the majority were for pushing on. As the bus crew already knew, we would arrive after dark, too late to cross the border. Group pressure finally prevailed, and off we set again. When we finally arrived at the Khunjrab there was, of course, no sign of our luggage.

In retrospect it is difficult to explain the collective abrogation of sanity by such a large and seasoned group of individual travellers. Everyone knows you never, never let yourself be separated from your luggage. Not only had we allowed this to happen, we had handed over our receipts as well. Well might one smirk, as others were to do at our subsequent discomfort. They of course would never have done anything so foolish.

In defence we can only argue we were lulled into a false sense of security by the fact that: firstly, the party was entirely comprised of foreigners. This was therefore not a scheduled run, but more like a group hire. We weren't, however, in any sense a real group except in our foreigness and our desire to cross over into Pakistan. Secondly, the bus office clerk spoke some English, a surprising accomplishment in Kashgar. Perhaps she was just brought in for the occasion. This maybe led us to believe the organisation was on the marginally higher level of efficiency associated with group tour travel. Thirdly, the bus was undoubtedly going to be overloaded with occupants, let alone luggage, therefore separate provision for it, in a truck we were assured would be accompanying us, seemed both logical and sensible. The truck in fact looked like it had a much better chance of completing the journey successfully than the bus. Fourthly, maybe it was simply the effect of the relaxed atmosphere in Kashgar. We were all tired after months of China travel and saw this journey as the final hurdle. Almost home, that is in a manner of speaking unless you come from Northern Pakistan. But then, isn't one most likely to fall at the last hurdle?

What little we could see in the dark was not very encouraging. A few managed to get accommodation in the guesthouse, some of us slept on the kitchen floor. A few hardy souls slept in the bus. Already an unpleasant atmosphere was developing. The Han bus crew were unfriendly and uncooperative, in no way apologetic for the very poor conditions. They made a great show of how considerate they were being providing some rough covering on the floor.

The Khunjrab Frontier Post is at about 14,000 feet and it snowed during the night. I had no warm clothing and passed a miserable night succumbing maybe to even more virulent attacks of 'Xinjiang belly'. Too late now to regret all those Kashgar bazaar excesses.

In the cold light of day things didn't look any better. By midday we had been through customs and immigration, but as we still had no luggage this was a bit of a sham. Customs seemed quite happy to clear us, although our bags could have been packed with valuable Chinese antiques. Perhaps they really do have a Chinese version of the second sight. On entering China all goods like cameras, watches, etc. are itemised and your receipt must be presented along with the items in question upon departure. As most of the goods weren't there to be checked they simply ignored this procedure. Once immigration control had stamped our passports we were technically no longer in China, the start of a period as stateless persons. There is a gap on my passport between being signed out of China and into Pakistan. Should this ever be investigated they might well wonder what I had been up to in this wild part of the world where China, Russia, Afghanistan, Pakistan and India all border within a few miles; shades perhaps of the Great Game. Had we in fact been engaged on some such enterprise this experience only proved that far from being romantic and exciting, the setting is uncomfortable and unrewarding.

At this stage a major debate took place. There was much ranting from the bus crew. Their idea was that they should drive us four hours over the border to Sost on the Pakistan side and leave us. Part of the problem, they explained, was that only the one driver had a passport. He was also supposed to drive the truck with the luggage when it came. He was at least making a reasonable point that he could not be expected to drive both vehicles at once. Being separated from our luggage in China was one thing, leaving it the other side of an international border quite another. This was not because I personally had any fears for the luggage being stolen. Hijacking a whole truckload of foreigners luggage would, I am sure,be a quick way to get yourself shot in China. But if we had left the country it would be next to impossible to exert any pressure. Who knows how long we might have to wait at the other end. We decided we would not leave without it.

There didn't appear to be a great deal else we could do in the meantime. If the bus was anywhere en route, and they were vague to the point of obscurity on the subject, it didn't seem likely it was going to appear in the next few hours. When I referred to the setting as being unrewarding and unromantic I was speaking in relation to the pursuit of espionage, etc. If we were to accept that there was nothing to be done, then attention could be given to what was actually there.

The Khunjrab Frontier Post lies about two-thirds of the way up the valley to the highest point which is the border line between China and Pakistan. By this stage the road has begun to benefit from some attention, but to either side is wilderness. At the post itself were compounds for the customs, the immigration, a Post/Public Security Office, a guesthouse, and the kitchen and a mean corrugated shack that were controlled by the bus company. Littered about was the usual mess, though fortunately this was not quite of Tibetan proportions, in all a rather squalid little encampment. The setting, though, was magnificent. To the west the Pamirs spiked the skyline with Russia and Afghanistan beyond. To the south lay the Karakoram, Pakistan and Kashmir.

With Una and Jacques, a young Swiss, I set off for the hills. Out on the plain we were joined by Nathalie, one of the French girls. From the border post west towards the Pamirs lies a wide valley sloping gently up to the foothills where a large Kirghiz herd was grazing. I had earlier noticed smoke from some way up a reentrant due west and was making for this. Where rivers come down from the snow fields the harsh brown gives way to pockets of lush grazing for the Kirghiz.

Passing through a veritable warren of marmots, inquisitive, only partly shy, we reached a Kirghiz encampment, six black yurts, cheese suspended on a blanket to dry , a few tethered goats. Some simple chanelling had been done to create a couple of delightful little ponds. No sign of any menfolk. Women and children peeping out from doorways. We both did and didn't want to intrude, so set off uphill again. A stiff climb for another hour brought us up to the snowline, which must have receded all of two thousand feet since the morning. The weather was beginning to close in but we were blessed with a view of glaciers reaching up to pointed peaks and a whole panorama back down the valley north towards Tashkurgan, with the grey snow clouds boiling up towards us. More of the same to the west, the south, the east. Enough. We were forced into a hasty retreat, following down one of the roaring rivers.

Passing back close to the yurts we were hailed by a Kirghiz man and on crossing over were invited into his yurt. These are constructed from skins and heavy cloth over stretched poles with a central smoke hole above a mud fire place. A woven coloured rug made a partitioned sleeping corner; the effect light and remarkably spacious inside. On one wall hung a snug cot with a tiny baby, designed almost as if to rock with the movement of the skins.

The large behatted man appeared to be the only male in residence. To support him were three generations of women, a wizened but tough looking granny, his wife, and two beautiful young girls. All were unveiled, only the younger child shy and holding back. Sadly we had no language in common. They plied us with bread, yoghurt and the most delicious cold cows milk.

I think the last I had tasted had been in London in February, and it's not quite the same out of a bottle. In return they wanted one of Nathalie's beads, which after considerable examination and haggling, no language needed, she agreed to part with.

The 1.5 million Kirghiz, a Mongoloid people originally from Siberia, migrated to the Pamirs in the ninth century, and have remained ever since in the highest inhabited plateau in the world. The exceptionally hard conditions, the constant search for pastures, have forced them into small bands of nomads, a few family groups moving together. Proud and independent, they have proved to be an intractable problem in the Soviet Russian drive for collectivisation. They are reputed to be the very fiercest of fighters.

By the time we got back to the post, the wind was up and snow was dusting the ground. Most of the party had taken refuge in the shack and were in the process of getting a fire going. It came as no surprise that there was still no sign of the luggage. Supper turned out to be a bowl of watery noodle soup for a monstrous 3 yuan and some bitter exchanges about paying for accommodation. After everyone had gone to bed a very unpleasant shouting match ensued with the bus company representative demanding four yuan a head. This was even more rapacious than the Tibetans. We all refused to pay as not only were we being cheated, but we had changed our Chinese money (it is useless outside the country). Officially we weren't in China anymore anyway. Their suggestion that we could pay in dollars was not well received. Most of all though, we resented being blackmailed to pay for shared filthy beds we were having to occupy because of their inefficiency.

Their credibility was already seriously undermined, having told us earlier within the space of an hour that (1) the truck had broken down, (2) it was due to arrive at 8 p.m., (3) they didn't know where it was. We speculated whether the truck had gone elsewhere for another deal, as it was only half-full with our luggage. Did the drivers get a cut the longer we were stuck and had to pay for meals and accommodation? Subsequently it was clear the truck was never going to travel direct to the border. Our luggage represented less than a quarter load. When it did finally arrive it carried half a dozen bicycles and a whole assortment of goods for cross-border trade.

These altercations ended with an attempt by the enemy, our captors even, as they now appeared, to throw me out in the snow. The issue at this juncture was finalised for the night by the offer of violence for violence. After all this excitement I slept quite soundly.

To get a picture of this stranded group think of a few national characteristics, exagerate them, forget them. Think about a few months of China travel. Imagine you are very tired, maybe in poor health, and now some of your worst fears are being realised, and you should have known better. So what are you going to do? Is this a group? If so can it all of a sudden find a group identity? You could be any of the following.

Three very clean young Germans, they had a minimal impact at least on me, besides wondering how they managed to stay so clean. Their pixie-suited compatriot had braved the Gyangtse monsoon without even getting a spot of mud on his clothing.

Two Dutch lads, light and humourous, always a pleasure to travel with.

Nancy, travelling with a serious tall bearded American who kept wanting to have democratic meetings to determine our plan of action, she, a West Coast environmental lawyer, the legal brain behind the hastily drafted letter of complaint and one of the sanest of the party. One might question whether sanity is an important quality in such circumstances.

Malcolm, the other member of the British sub-clique, suffering some frustration, this being about the longest he had been in one place since leaving Australia a few months previously. Guzzling bottles of wine, scoffing tins of pork and straightforwardly outspoken about the best course of action to take – "string the little bastards up" – if the slit eyes weren't going to oblige, the pompous American prig, Nancy's companion, would do just as well in his estimation.

Nathalie and Violaine, French, of course, solidly gallic, enjoying themselves and well adapted to the patience required for survival in China travel.

The very smart Italian couple, superbly equipped with down jackets, quite appallingly fashionable, though possibly slightly wasted in the present circumstances. On the other hand I am sure it was good for morale. They were a bit anxious about catching their flight from Karachi, but didn't let this show.

An Australian family, a rather emaciated and harrassed looking artist with his wife and seven and nine year old sons. They had been travelling with their children for several years, so were no strangers to the game, although China is not an easy place to travel with children of this age. She appeared to be suffering a little from altitude sickness and we were still supposed to be going up. (A Dutch homeopathic doctor I had met in Kashgar had managed to get an ambulance down from the border when they were stuck coming in from Pakistan by feigning an attack, but presumably this only works if you want to go down. It doesn't make your luggage appear.)

An American girl – Mary Ellen type, had subjected us to a nonstop commentary from the moment we left Kashgar even to the extent of offering the driver gratuitous and spurious advice as to how to drive his bus. She was accompanied by an English TEFL teacher on his way back from Japan but I didn't get much of an impression of him as he rarely managed to get a word in edgeways.

A manic overseas Chinese chef from Hong Kong and America who furiously juggled lenses throughout the bus trip. He spoke very much better Putonghua than I did, but he shared the native reticence in relation to accepting a leadership role, and like Malcolm, having sensibly kept his luggage with him, he took the first opportunity to remove himself on a Pakistani bus.

Two Japanese, amused, apparently unconcerned, appreciative of any efforts made jointly on their behalf. No face lost on their part.

The Cambridge student, spent the entire time in dispute with any Chinese he could find, much of it with the P.S.B. who were not in the least bit interested in what he had to say since they couldn't understand him. He demanded to be put through to the British Embassy in Beijing. It was no great surprise that he was not successful, as were his attempts to hire a jeep to take him to Tashkurgan to search for his luggage. Since he wouldn't listen to anybody else's advice he didn't attract a great deal of sympathy. If anything he became the cruel butt of our own jokes, a deplorable lack of solidarity, but then he was hardly acting with a 'cool' British head. The fundamental problem, I believe, was that he had come in from Pakistan to Kashgar and was now on his way out again, (he simply hadn't addressed himself to the art of the possible in China.) For those who had already had their 'baptism of fire', it was easier to view the proceedings with some equanimity.

On the morning of the 29th I made the rounds, trying to enlist some aid, anybody's, in sorting out our predicament. At the immigration unit the soldier on duty did not want to indentify the unit leader. This would have been bad news for him as the bearer of bad tidings. After a great deal of persuasion he was finally located. Questions about how we might contact our embassies were not well received, as was expected and intended. Again we were assured the truck was on its way.

I suggested they might like to phone to find out where the truck might be, but they claimed there was no way they could find this out, and anyway the phone was out of order. It was obviously one of those situations where challenging this last statement or pointing out the illogicality of their knowing the truck was on the way if they could not phone, was not going to get us any further. Having now marked my man, though, I asked him directly to help us. Two hours later I tracked him down again, and with a laugh he told me the truck had broken down at Bulukou. When I asked whether he could find out anymore for us he stated he had already helped us (how wasn't clear) and that it was no longer any of his business.

In a country where taking the initiative was positively discouraged for many years no one wants to accept responsibility, or be labelled a leader, unless their liability is strictly defined and limited. A classic example of this was displayed by the different *danwei* (work units), immigration, customs, guesthouse and bus company. In our estimation the bus company was clearly at fault, but the only real assistance we were able to elicit was from the Uyghur in charge of the guesthouse. Eventually it appeared he had some overall responsibity for the frontier post as the resident senior cadre.

I had a couple of years previously made approaches to a

number of travel companies to sound out the possibility of courier/guidework in China. I little expected to find that by default, as the only member of the party with any pretence to be able to speak Chinese, that I would be labelled by the Chinese themselves as a tour group leader for a party of twenty-six foreigners from ten different countries. Could this be my finest hour? Years of training in military and social work skills, with a smattering of language thrown in, all bought to fruition on the Chinese border. Would there be an international incident?

The previous evening and again in the morning there had been a discussion of tactics and it had been generally agreed that we should register a formal complaint. Having failed miserably at immigration, contact was made about midday with the guesthouse danwei leader, and our grievances were put to him. To my great surprise he suggested we go ahead and write our complaint. He appeared genuinely concerned about our welfare as well as the poor image portrayed of the People's Republic. I had pushed this for all it was worth.

The next thing we knew we were being treated to a half-decent meal for two yuan. Three bottles of wine were even produced which quickly disappeared in a number of toasts. This with rice, aubergines, peppers and a little mutton represented, under the cirumstances, a veritable banquet.

The sort of situation, delays, uncertainty, hunger and discomfort that would have produced almost instant apoplexy on arrival in China, now seemed like a rather trying day or two's delay and most of the party calmly dozed away a few hours in the afternoon sun – *putao jiu* (wine) assisted.

A passing Italian tour group very kindly gave us their remaining 60 RMB which paid for the meal, and Dutch and American couples coming in from Pakistan gave some watermelons which tasted wonderful (after a few days in Kashgar I had become almost bored with them). Best of all, a new experience was a bag of fresh Hunza apricots. Sadly the season appeared already to be over, and this was the only taste forthcoming.

The danwei chief further told us the bus and truck would arrive together between four and six and leave that night.

Our bus had left earlier that morning when we had refused to pay 180 yuan a day to keep it at the frontier post, the original driver being so ill he had to be rushed down to a lower altitude. I can't say we felt much sympathy for him.

We were generally lulled into a false sense of security by this change in attitude, and almost believed that transport would duly arrive. Genuine or not, it was a masterly performance by the chief. As the light began to fade it became obvious that even if transport came the border would be closed. A surprise change of heart by the bus company party produced more noodle soup. Everyone found a bed of sorts, mainly at the guesthouse for 10 yuan. Argumentative to the last I got this reduced to 7 yuan with my Yunnan ID – a principal still at stake.

In the morning the Dong Feng turned up around 9 a.m. However it took until 2 p.m. before we finally crossed the border in a Pakistani bus, having obtained a 25 yuan refund from the bus company which they fought over to the last. Everyone was so relieved to be reunited with their luggage that they took the final round of arguments and delays without any conspicuous loss of temper.

The danwei chief was keen to hear my view on any improvements they could make in their service, but I'm not sure how much he took in of my lecture on business responsibility, although one of the customs officers, a local Tadjik, made a very good job of translation (three years at the Shanghai Customs School he informed me).

As we drove out past the immigration pole most indicated their negative feelings about the treatment of the last few days with a series of boos and catcalls. For me this was a sad and comtemplative moment. China had been my home for the last six months and on balance I had little to complain about. If the last drop of blood had been extracted before being allowed on my way – so be it. I bore no ill will, even the border fiasco had not been without amusement and compensations. How else would I have visited a Kirghiz yurt. The shared vicissitudes had also brought a new set of travelling companions.

It is on its outer edges that China is most insecure. They have been so wrapped up in their own internal affairs, in creating a new China from the old, it is hardly surprising some of their organisations are lacking in finesse, their responses appearing unfriendly. Progress doesn't happen overnight, it has to be learnt and experienced.

Out in no man's land we passed a couple of army checkpoints and were joined by some P.L.A. men joy-riding on the back of the bus. For almost two hours we ground uphill in our flashy Nissan 'monarch of the road' to the two pillars erected to mark the border at 15,420 feet and to commemorate the opening and building of the Karakoram highway. Here we stopped for a quick photocall and then plunged headlong down the Pakistani side past towering rock faces, rushing streams, hairpin bends and a series of all too briefly glimpsed views up steep valleys to sweeping glaciers. Throughout the conductor hung out of the open back door riding shotgun – more Wild West antics appropriate to the surroundings.

13

PAKISTAN

THE HUNZA VALLEY

My first taste of Pakistan was a passport checking post where we stopped for tea and ravenously devoured biscuits. The tea came in a supersaturated sugary solution known as 'chai', specially designed to put the last finishing touches to my crumbling dentistry. The culture shock of moving into the ex-Empire is overwhelming. The military, in particular, appear to have undergone little change other than the absence of British officers. There is an air of efficiency with plenty of crisp uniforms and smart badges. The people are polite, friendly, even deferential. This is a society which makes no pretence of equality.

At Sost it took a couple of hours before the bus went on, although clearing immigration and customs took about ten minutes. A few refugee tents lay scattered about with lettering denoting their donation from the EEC, a reminder that there was a war going on not far away over the hills.

From Sost it is a two hour hus ride on down hill past Passu and the Batura glacier to KarimAbad. As the glacier is constantly on the move downhill, so is the road, which regularly washes out altogether. At the best of times it requires some skilled driving to negotiate the rushing melt water coursing out from under the glacier carrying a mountain of debris in its path. Sadly the light was fading, rapidly obscuring superb scenery of golden wheat fields and green orchards with a backdrop of the staggeringly rugged surroundings of mountains still in formation.

Our fellow bus passengers were a cheerful lot, despite the fact that several of them had been turned back at the border because they lacked the correct documentation to take dollars out of the country. They would apparently have to go all the way back to Lahore and start all over again. Kashgar has the reputation of sin city, and it was rumoured the Pakistanis escaped from the rigidity of Islamic society for a holiday of drink and brothels in Kashgar. If this is true it is an odd reflection on Communist China, usually noted for its high moral tone.

The bus provided an opportunity for several of the Pakistanis to try out their English on us. In between bursts of patriotic singing along the lines of 'I love beautiful Pakistan', we bandied back and forth our only common area of language, 'Botham' (which they pronounced as 'Bottom' with a slightly sinister silent h), accompanied by one of those gestures of the forearm that would no doubt have appealed to the man himself. 'Imran Khan-Botham, Imran Khan-Botham'. I thought of trying Kapil Dev, and then couldn't remember whether he played for Pakistan or India, not a mistake I wanted to make under the circumstances so "Botham-Imran Khan" had to do.

We arrived in Karim-Abad in the dark and opted for a jeep ride up the narrow winding track to be dropped off at the New Tourist Hunza Inn. What joy, how civilised to be able to sit down and relax with an excellent curry followed by a very comfortable night in a tent, there being no rooms available – a tent though, better appointed than most Chinese guesthouses, with clean sheets, a bedside lamp, and waking to the incomparable view from the front flap of Rakaposhi rising sheer 25,500 feet across the valley, the morning sun reflecting back pure gold. I won't attempt to outdo my travelling predecessors in eulogistic excesses. To see is to believe.

A day of blissful recuperative ease followed, bathed in the surrounding beauty, absorbing its rejuvenating atmosphere. I was particularly amused to find that the natives with any English really did sound like Peter Sellers doing Indian impersonations. This coupled with the unimaginable luxury of porridge, fried eggs, toast, jam and tea for breakfast, made me seriously question whether I hadn't popped through some time warp into one of 'Roger's Ripping Tales From The Raj'. Should I have been worrying, Peter Fleming style, about whether I could get a pair of trousers decently pressed in order not to let the side down?

The next day I walked, or more accurately scrambled, up to the Ultar Glacier. Both Ben and Una turned back but Jaques arrived about an hour later having dangerously negotiated his way up the glacier bed, which he described as something of a terrifying ordeal, with the surface breaking up all around him and shoots of stones whistling past. From the idyllic spot where I had stopped to sunbathe and watch a couple of shepherds shearing, the main flow of the glacier was invisible. I had scrambled up well to the side and it was only from this vantage point that I realised the main part of the glacier lay below me. What I could see was a subsidiary, cascading down the mountainside like lava. The surface was almost coal black in places, so at first I did not recognise it as a glacier at all.

From the time that we left the Baltit fort, which dominates Karim-Abad, to the start of the steepest part of the scramble up the side of the glacier, we had followed an ingeniously constructed series of irrigation channels, these often literally built onto the cliff face skirting round waterfalls. By this means the whole of the Hunza Valley below is irrigated. Even through long periods of drought there is always water flowing from the slowly receding glaciers on both sides of the valley, ensuring the future of this fertile region.

Hunza is rightly famous for its apricots. It is said that, at the time they ripen, the smell of rotting fruit is overpowering, the natural production far exceeding the harvest. With the coming of the road this will doubtless all change rapidly. The impact of tourism will also begin to be felt, but the people have a proud history of independence and didn't get the feeling that they were about to be overwhelmed.

Hunza also has a reputation for longevity, and some preliminary field studies have suggested that there is an almost total absence of many of the stress related illnesses of the West. On only the briefest aquaintance I felt this would be an easy place in which to find peace of mind. Some attribute longevity in part to the water. The most notable feature of it, as far as I could see, was that it carried a lot of micre, making fantastic patterns glittering in the sunshine as it swirled along the irrigation channels. Maybe they referred to 'Hunza water', the local wine, which unfortunately we didn't manage to sample. Pakistan is a dry country. In Hunza, though, as Ismaelis, followers of the Aga Khan, alcohol has not traditionally been strictly forbidden. Recently the Aga Khan ruled that both drinking and smoking were not conducive to a pure life. Cigarettes were unobtainable in Karim-Abad, but the local wine we were told was not outlawed, merely discouraged.

In general this is a much more relaxed form of Islam. The women are for the most part unveiled, common sense for working in the fields as much as anything. The Aga Khan Foundation pumps money into a whole range of educational, social and economic institutions; health centres, primary schools, etc. and is undoubtedly a major force in the area.

I had heard the tales of the odd blue eyed blonde person in this part of the world, a legacy of Alexander the Great, the Kaffirs, who knows? But I had hardly been prepared to meet so many redheads. One such teenage girl with a shawl over her head, barefooted, could have been a 'Morag of the Glens' stepping out of a Highland crofting scene.

That evening an English traveller who had been in the same dormitory in Kashgar arrived at the New Tourist Inn. He confirmed that the 'Pirelli Incident' had already been reported back to Kashgar. For some reason the Khunjrab border post is known, certainly among the travelling community as Pirelli, though nowhere have I seen this written. For me at least, but I suspect for the other unfortunates at the border as well, Pirelli has for all time lost its association with tyres.

Our informant had been at Tashkurgan the night before the truck left. He reported that before the truck had even set out from Kashgar there had been a heated arument between the Pakistanis and the bus company. They refused to pay excess for luggage transported by lorry. This would appear to have been a long running dispute. The Pakistanis had been making the most of the trading opportunities that had opened up with the opening of the border, loading the maximum onto the Chinese cross-border buses, which as already observed had quite enough trouble coping with passengers. Unfortunately our luggage appears to have been caught up in the showdown.

When our truck had finally reached Tashkurgan a bus had broken down at Bulukou and the preceding bus had gone back from Tashkurgan, so we were no doubt also affected by the knock-on from this, and this may explain why they were so keen to get our bus back down from Khunjrab. No great consolation though to receive this information after the event.

In the morning, fortified with more porridge, an absurd start to another day of great heat, I accompanied Ben and Jacques down the hill to the Karakoram highway. In the valley an impressive bridge spans the river with very Chinese looking lions on the parapet. They obviously had a hand in the construction somewhere. By the roadside a sign in Urdu and English states 'Relax'. 'Pay Attention' might be more appropriate for most of the manic drivers. This apparently is the all clear sign after a series of threatened landslides.

Our goal for the morning was the site of some ancient petraglyphs carved by early Buddhist pilgrims en route from China. There was not a great deal to see. The Pakistani Tourist Board, or whatever the equivalent organisation is, didn't seem overenthusiastic or informative about them. A nearby sign reads, 'these marks were made about the time the area became holy to the local population'.

The rest of the day was spent scrambling up through terracing, water courses and a profusion of rich vegetation. To cap it all the sun set pink on Rakaposhi. Sitting down to the regulation evening curry we were joined by a couple of French photojournalists working for Geo magazine on an article on the Karakoram highway. They were a fund of information on the route, particularly on the racial and linguistic groupings that cross several borders. In Hunza they speak Brushuski, which is thought to be related to no known Indo-European language, whereas further up the valley the Tadjiks occupy both sides of the border, with a shared language and culture. Pre-1949 there was effectively no border with regard to trade, marriage, etc.

The French couple had chanced upon a tale of the Emir of Hunza's nephew whose family had owned property as far afield as Yarkand. Since the recent relaxations he had made approaches about family properties in Yarkand and had been most surprised when it was indicated that these properties could now be reclaimed. If this is indeed true it goes very much further than simply allowing a degree of regional autonomy or encouraging the return of private enterprise in China.

We left for Gilgit on a dark dawn with a ride door to door to the Golden Peak Hotel. There is almost a mechanical rhythm to the way one is processed by the family business from place to place, inevitably meeting up with the same travellers over and over again. The circuit doesn't simply apply to China.

The route down from Hunza is spectacular, but the excellence of the engineering of the highway had I felt rendered it less impressive than it must have been in former days. John Keay's account of the route in the 1890's in 'The Gilgit Game' suggests it was a major obstacle even to troops well accustomed to traversing difficult passes. Much of the campaigning around this area like the Hunza – Nagar battle in 1891 was inspired more by pursuit of the 'Great Game' than by any need, or desire, to control or pacify the local population. It also had much to do with bored young officers looking for a scrap. Not just some adventure to alleviate the tedium of regimental soldiering, but the chance to win glory and recognition, one of the few paths to accelerated promotion. The one thing this particular battle proved above all was that the passes were simply not feasible for large scale military operations, and certainly not viable for a Russian advance into Kashmir, a point that was not lost on the Russian minister who commented, *"Ils ont fermé la porte au nez"*.

In the evening they just happened to be having a polo practice. The distinct impression was that polo matches take place all the time. If anywhere is the natural home of polo, then Gilgit is it. To claim that it was atmospheric would be an understatement. Rays of evening sun shone through the trees, horses stampeded up and down in clouds of dust from light to shadow. On a couple of haystacks under the trees sat a party happily smoking away, while below them a band with two *suona* (shawm) and two drums beat out an excited rhythm. When a goal was scored the tempo increased to a frenzy. They subtly indicated when they thought the action seemed to be flagging. From time to time a couple of men danced in front of the band in what appeared to be an intoxicated trance, oblivious to the horses thundering past.

Spectators were lined right along the stone walls on either side only two to three feet above the action. This at times was carried out at alarmingly close quarters with a melee of players flailing their sticks wildly. This must surely be one of the most dangerous spectator sports, and to our enquiries on this subject we were indeed informed that accidents to both riders and spectators were not uncommon. Ali, the owner of the Golden Peak Hotel turned out to be one of the star players and cut a real dash with a bandage above his left eye from just such a recent polo accident.

Both riders and horses were magnificent, the whole spectacle the very essence of the male macho on which this society is based. The stratification in society is also very much in evidence. Servants hold spare sticks, run onto the pitch 'at considerable danger to themselves to retrieve dropped ones and then dutifully walk the horses up and down at halftime. We had noticed earlier in the day how in the bank the distasteful task of emptying an ashtray or bringing tea was strictly confined to specific individuals. My knowledge was insufficient to determine exactly how this stratification or caste was defined, but its operation was unmistakeable.

The colour of the skin may have changed, but in essence the Raj is still here. The polo players were for the most part army and police officers. Even when heavily subsidised polo has never been a poor man's game. And whose was the son I met crossing the bridge in grey trousers, white shirt, blazer and tie?

From here on my homeward journey was downhill all the way, taking first the easy option of the flight from Gilgit to

Islamabad. All internal flights are heavily subsidised. At £8 this is definitely a bargain, particularly if you like your aerial views dramatic and at close quarters. The wings practically clip the hill side on take off and for much of the journey you appear to fly in the valley rather than above it. Below and beside rush terraces and river valleys slashed into the mountainside. The *piece de resistance*, Nanga Parbat, was in cloud, but by this stage I was more interested in green valleys than more snowy peaks. Dervla Murphy quotes herself in Gilgit in 1963 returning in 1974, 'this was the wrong approach to a noble range. One should win the privilege of looking down on such a scene, and because I had done nothing to earn a glimpse of these remote beauties I felt that I was cheating'. For once I felt I had earned just such a treat.

A couple of days in Rawalpindi and I travelled on by rail with Una, twenty six sweltering hours to Karachi. At least Pakistani 'Hard Seat' means a seat. In Karachi we picked up a flight via Istanbul. Unable to get the flight we had wanted we had left the travel agents bound for a country neither of us had ever remotely considered visiting before.

Turkey was a mindless week of recuperation, adjustment halfway east to west, a cultural decompression chamber. I felt reassuringly well on the way to detachment. This was soon to be put back in perspective, however, when the flight from Istanbul was delayed 1½ hours. This seemed infinitely more frustrating than days of waiting on Asiatic travels. Already I was starting to think like an alienated Westerner again. Is the veneer so thin?

A week after I reached home I completed the final metamorphosis to becoming a Chinaman by turning yellow. I discovered the true meaning of holding a jaundiced view of the world with the ravages of Hepatitis A. It is, of course, debatable whether I wouldn't have done my liver more damage had I been free to wine and dine on traveller's tales. At least it enforced a contemplative slow down and an opportunity to commit some of the previous months to paper.

———————————■———————————

BIBLIOGRAPHY

Charles Allan	A Mountain in Tibet, Futura 1983
Arrian	The Campaigns of Alexander, 1958.
John F Avelon	In Exile from the Land of Snows, Wisdom 1984
F.M. Bailey	No Passport to Tibet, Rupert Hart-Davis, London 1957
Chris Bonnington	Kongar, China's Elusive Summit, Hodder 1982
Elizabeth B Booz	Tibet, A Guide To Being There, Hong Kong 1986
M Buckley, R Strauss	Tibet Survival Guide, Lonely Planet 1986
Mildred Cable with Francesca French	The Gobi Desert, Hodder, London 1942
Ian Cameron	Mountains Of The Gods, Century, 1984
Edmund Candler	The Unveiling of Lhasa, Nelson, 1905
Spencer Chapman	Lhasa, The Holy City, Chatto, 1940
Bruce Chatwin	The Songlines, Picador, London 1988
Suydam Cutting	The Fire Ox and Other Years, Collins, 1947
Nigel Danziger	Danzigers Travels, Paladin, 1988
H H P Deasy	In Tibet and Chinese Turkestan, Fisher Unwin, 1901
Vicomte D'Ollone	In Forbidden China, T. Fisher Unwin, London 1912
C.P. Fitzgerald	The Birth of Communist China, Penguin, 1964
Peter Fleming	Bayonets To Lhasa, Rupert Hart-Davis, 1961
Peter Fleming	The Siege Of Peking, Rupert Hart-Davis, 1959
Peter Fleming	News From Tartary, Rupert Hart-Davis, 1959
Robert Ford	Captured in Tibet, George Harrap, 1957
Stuart and Roma Gelder	The Timely rain, Travels in New Tibet, Hutchinson 1964
Lama Anagaika Govinda	The Way Of The White Clouds, Rider & Co., 1984
Peter Goullart	Forgotten Kingdom, John Murray, 1955
Heinrich Harrer	Seven Years in Tibet, Rupert Hart-Davis, 1953
Peter Hopkirk	Trespassers On The Roof Of The World, OUP, 1982
Peter Hopkirk	Trespassers On The Silk road, OUP, 1982
John Keay	Where Men And Mountains Meet, John Murray, 1977
John Keay	The Gilgit Game, John Murray, 1979

171

David Kellog	In Search of China, Shipman, 1989
The Dalai Lama	My Land and My People, Weidenfeld, 1962.
Harold Lamb	Ghengis Khan, 1928
P. Somerville Large	To the Navel of the World, Hamish Hamilton, 1987
Ronald Latham	Marco Polo, The Travels, Penguin, 1958
Tieh-Tseng Li	Tibet, Today and Yesterday, Bookman, New York 1960
Tom Longstaff	This My Voyage, John Murray, 1950
Ella Maillart	Forbidden Journey, Heineman, 1927
Fosco Maraini	Secret Tibet, Hutchinson, London 1954
Peter Mathieson	The Snow Leopard, Chatto 1979
Andre Migot	Tibetan Marches, Hart-Davis, 1956
Timothy Mo	An Insular Possession, Chatto, 1986
Geoffrey Moorhouse	To The Frontier, Hodder Stoughton, 1984
Dervla Murphy	Where the Indus is Young, John Murray, 1977
Alexander David-Neel	With Magicians And Mystics In Tibet, Rider & Co., 1931
Alexander David-Neel	Initiations And Initiates In Tibet, Rider & Co., 1931
Alexander David-Neel	My Journey to Lhasa, Heineman, London 1927
George Paterson	Tibetan Journey, Faber & Faber, 1956
E.O. Reischauer and J.K. Fairbank	East Asia, The Great Tradition, Houghton Mifflin, 1958
Hugh Richardson	Tibet and its History, Shambala, 1984
Alan Samagalski and Michael Buckley	China, A Travel Survival Kit, Lonely Planet, 1984
Franz Schurmann and Orville Schell	China Readings 1, Imperial China, 2, Republican China China Readings 3, Communist China, Penguin, 1967
Vickram Seth	From Heaven's Lake, Chatto, 1983
W.D. Shakabpa	Tibet. A Political History, Potala, New York, 1984
Eric Shipton	That Untravelled World, Lonely Planet
Eric Shipton	The Six Mountain Travel Books, Diadem, 1985
Sir Aurel Stein	On Ancient Central Asian Tracks, MacMillan, 1933
Paul Theroux	Riding the Iron Rooster, Hamish Hamilton, 1988
Colin Thubron	Behind the Wall, Heineman, 1987
Chogyam Trungpa	The Sacred Path of the Warrior, Shambala, 1984
L. Austine Waddell	Lhasa and its Mysteries, John Murray, London 1905
Sorrel Wilby	Tibet, Queen Anne Press, London 1988
G R C Worcester	The Junkman Smiles, Chatto, 1959
Zhang Xianliang	Half of Man is Woman, Viking, 1988

172

A NOTE ON
TRANSLITERATION

The transliteration of Chinese place names has always posed considerable problems. None of the systems of romanisation adopted resolve all of these. For the most part I have used the pinyin romanisation adopted throughout Communist China after 1949. As China has reopened her doors in the last few years this system has come to be used increasingly in the West, and so is more familiar now for many readers than Yale, Wade-Giles or any of the other systems in vogue in the past. The pinyin system, however, has not been adopted by the overseas Chinese with the result that there is a most effective cultural and political break between the two – they cannot read each others propaganda, which is probably no bad thing.

This process was also carried into simplifying the characters on the mainland, in the interests of greater literacy. In achieving this goal they have been remarkably successful, but many purists argue that the beauty of the written language has thus been seriously undermined. Fortunately as this is written in English this particular argument does not concern us.

Where formerly the Nationalist capital city was written Chungking, it is now Chongqing. A further complication is introduced in Tibet. The second city is usually written in the Western atlases as Shigatze, the pinyin transliteration would be Rikaze. In these cases I have preferred the former system, the latter only being intelligible or identifiable by a student of Chinese, and probably a fairly pedantic one at that. Similarly in Xinjiang (Sinkiang) I refer to the frontier post at Khunjrab, few people would make much of Hongqilafu. If all this seems very confusing, it is. It is not helped by the original transliterations in the West from the accounts of early explorers, who often had little idea where they were, where they had been, or what any of the places were really called. Chinese is an homophonous language, that is it has a limited range of sounds, or phonemes, many of which to an untrained ear are indistinguishable one from another.

All in all one can be excused for finding the whole matter of rendering Chinese into English fraught with pitfalls. It is best to regard it as a matter of fun rather than a problem, the same approach that has to be adopted in the interests of sanity in China travel.

Money in China comes in two different forms, FEC – Foreign Exchange Certificates, and RMB – Renminbi (people's currency). The latter is the internal currency and is non-transferable. FEC is specifically for foreigners and for regulating foreign exchange. It provides access to certain rationed goods in special stores, and is consequently much saught after. The black market exchange has varied from 110 RMB for 100 FEC up to 180. The smallest denomination in FEC is 1 Jiao (formal) or Mao, in RMB 1 Fen. 10 Fen = 1 Mao, 10 Mao = 1 Yuan (formal) or Kuai. 1 Kuai = 20p approx in 1986.

INDEX

PHOTOGRAPHS

1. Kunming backstreet.
2. Gold finial on Jokhang roof. Lhasa.
3. Young beggars in the Barkhor. Lhasa.
4. Roof courtyard in the Jokhang. Lhasa.
5. Bridge to Gomulingka. Lhasa.
6. Clockwise circumambulation of the Barkhor. Lhasa.
7. Gold centrepiece, roof of Jokhang. Lhasa.
8A. Triple image of Tsong Khapa at Ganden Monastery.
8B. 'Mao is out'. Roof of Ramoche. Lhasa.
9. Drogpa shepherdess at hot springs. Coquen.
10. An offering of juniper incense above Ganden.
11. Ganden Monastery. Founded 1417 – destroyed 1960's.
12. Dong and Geleng practice. Ganden.
13. New hands for Buddhas. Ganden.
14. Gyangtse main street after the monsoon.
15. Prayer-wheel wall on pilgrim circuit. Shigatze.
16. Horses at Chang Tang truckstop.
17. Drogpa boy with discarded rum bottle. Tunghu.
18. Drogpa at Mt Kailas.
19. Old Drogpa at salt lake. Tunghu.
20. Khampa pilgrims on truck to Kailas.
21. The valley of Amitabha. Kailas.
22. Pilgrim mother and children at Kailas river crossing.
23. Drogpa women at Kailas.
24. Kailas. North face.
25. Truck race back to Ali.
26. Khampas on Kailas pilgrimage.
27. Yurts near Gartok.
28. Villagers of Kokyar. Taklamakan.
29. Card school. Kashgar.
30. The timber market. Kashgar.
31. Melon feast. Yingkisha.
32. The author leaving China by the back door. Khunjrab.

———————————————— ■ ————————————————

With very many thanks – on the road, to Helen, Paulo and Wang Ruopeng in Dali; Liz in Kaifeng and Chengdu; Dave and Rebecca in Lhasa; Bill and Denise to Ali; Zop and Peta round Mt Kailas; Una, Ben and Jacques at Khunjrab; and in Kunming, to – Leslie, Lydia, Cynthia, Kim and Anne, Li Qiuming, Gayle and Harold Ma. For the initial encouragement, Monica Clough, to my Mother for nursing and constructive criticism, to Patricia for much inspiration and to Lalage Williams for word processing.

Maps by Ryszard Hajdul. All Photographs by the Author.

Set in Monotype Imprint by PTPS Norwich.